ROOMS NEAR CHANCERY LANE

THE PATENT OFFICE UNDER THE COMMISSIONERS, 1852-1883

By JOHN HEWISH

THE BRITISH LIBRARY

Rooms near Chancery Lane: The Patent Office under the Commissioners, 1852-1883
ISBN 0-7123-0853-9

Published by
The British Library
96 Euston Road
London NW1 2DB

British Library Cataloguing-in-Publication Data

A catalogue record for this book is available from The British Library

Desktop publishing by Concerto, Leighton Buzzard, Bedfordshire.
Tel: 01525 378757

Printed by Hobbs the Printers Ltd, Totton, Hampshire SO40 3YS

Contents

Preface

In April 1991, The Patent Office was relocated from London to Newport, South Wales. The connection with the capital, which had lasted since the Office was first established as an independent entity in 1852, was not quite severed however. The Office retains a presence in London for the receipt of applications, and until June 1999 this was still situated at the old Patent Office building at 25 Southampton Buildings, Chancery Lane, premises which were shared with the Science Reference and Information Service of The British Library (formerly The Patent Office Library).

The vacation of 25 Southampton Buildings both by The Patent Office and by The British Library is suitably marked by the publication of this interesting book, which tells the story of the early years of The Patent Office and the establishment of the patent system as an important way of supporting innovation. It will prove a fascinating read for both the specialist and the general reader.

Brian B Caswell
Assistant Director (Marketing)
The Patent Office
Newport
South Wales

Foreword

It is fitting that this book is written now as 25 Southampton Buildings, Chancery Lane, London, the home of the Patent Office and the Patent Office Library for the best part of 150 years, is their home no longer. The locality has an even longer association with the issuing of patents as it has housed chambers for Chancery officers since the seventeenth century and patent agents for almost as long. In 1991 the Patent Office moved most of its operations (including the Trade Marks and Designs Registries) from London to Newport, South Wales, leaving only a few functions on the original site and this rump, too, has now moved. The Patent Office Library, known at various times in its later history as the National Reference Library of Science and Invention, the Science Reference Library and, currently, the Science Reference and Information Service of the British Library, moved to the new site of the British Library at St Pancras, London in mid-1999. It has joined other parts of the Library such as the former British Museum Library, with its own Victorian legacy.

The book weaves a tale of considerable achievements under the Commissioners but at the same time reveals some extraordinary goings-on. Certain officials failed to distinguish public from private money. Financial irregularities and conflict between the two senior officials led to Government enquiry and censure involving the Lord Chancellor and other prominent figures. In all it shows the varied history of a public office in Victorian Britain.

This book represents many years of diligent research by the author. It provides a fitting testimony to the Patent Office and Patent Office Library as catalysts of innovation at the time that these institutions adapt to the next millennium in rooms removed from Chancery Lane.

David Newton
Head of Patents Information, British Library
Winter 1999

A note on the sources

To the best of my knowledge there is no sequential body of primary records for the Patent Office in the 19th century. The only approximation to one is the set of records for the Commissioners of Patents Museum at South Kensington from the 1850s to 1883. These letter-books, inventories and other papers were handed over with the collections and are now in the Science Museum Library and Document Centre. They give some idea of what must have been lost.

As regards official published papers the situation is very different: the several Select Committee and Royal Commission enquiries into patent law, the Library and Museum and the Edmunds affair make the Office surely one of the most investigated public offices of all time. Its having its own Library has also helped record survival: many of such archives as exist are now part of the British Library science collections.

The Patent Commissioners' annual reports to Parliament are indeed a sequence but are rather disappointing; they are mainly restricted to patent statistics and accounts, with occasional information on appointments, publications and the Library. Though signed only by the four Commissioners, this seems to have been a mere endorsement, the pen or voice is that of Woodcroft and his staff. The 1866 Report was used to publish the Treasury Solicitor's final report on the Edmunds case, making for once an – in this context – highly personal and inappropriate attack on the former Clerk of the Patents. It was issued to the Press but unlike the other Edmunds reports, never got into the Parliamentary Papers. Other published sources include the *Patent Journal* and the Commissioners Rules, Circulars and other notices.

Some records for the 19th century have survived in the Patent Office, more it seems through the individual concern of members of staff than through official action. The staff records are particularly complete. There are references in official and private papers to Bennet Woodcroft's journal or minute book. It is lost, but transcripts and notes from it exist.

It is impossible to give sources for all the various information that goes to make a book. The Public Record Office series of Treasury and Board of Trade papers both contain valuable material: the survival of the bulky Hindmarch and Greenwood papers on the Edmunds case was a pleasant surprise such as the PRO sometimes produces. The Royal Archives at Windsor contain evidence of Prince Albert's interest in the founding of the Office and its Museum. There is more material on the Museum in the archives of the Royal Commission on the 1851 Exhibition. I have looted James Harrison's many articles in specialist patent journals, *The Royal Society of Arts Journal* and the *Patent Office Examining Staff Magazine*, the 19th century technical press, especially *The Engineer* and *Engineering* provide the only running commentary on the Office affairs, though not always a balanced one.

Finally, no-one writing about the Patent Office now can ignore *Patent Office Centenary* (1952). Its author Herbert Harding (1884–1976) was the first of those who did what they could unofficially to save surviving records. His 48 pages are a model of concision and relevance. Acquaintance with his papers increases one's respect for him.

Acknowledgments

My particular thanks are due to James Harrison and Dr R.T. Smith for advice, the loan of papers, and a shared interest in Patent Office history over many years. Also to Mandy Taylor and Tony Vincent of the Science Museum Library and Documentation Centre respectively. John Dugnolle, Honorary Archivist of the Patent Office and Brian Caswell, Marketing Manager, have both given willing assistance, the latter in negotiating a generous grant towards publication. I am grateful to Dr David Newton for giving the text his imprimatur and last but not least to other former colleagues in the British Library.

Acknowledgment is also due to Rupert Hart Davis for permission to quote from *The Letters of A.E. Housman*, ed. H. Maas; to Oxford University Press for excerpts from *The Gladstone Diaries*, vol 6, ed. H.G. Matthews; to the Librarian of Trinity College, Cambridge for the use of correspondence relating to A.E. Housman; to HM The Queen and the Royal Archives for letters and minutes from Bennet Woodcroft's meetings with the Prince Consort and to The Patent Office for quotation from *Patent Office Centenary* and *A Century of Trademarks*.

Introduction

In October 1852 a new public office opened in London to administer a reformed system of patents for inventions.

The establishment of a single office for the purpose was itself a reform; the name Patent Office, or Great Seal Patent Office had applied to several addresses in London since at least the 17th century. As far as inventions were concerned the new office replaced an earlier Lord Chancellor's Patent Office and much of the work of the Law Officers' Patent Bill Office. Both had been part of the notoriously elaborate and recently satirised Chancery system for granting all letters patent.

Though the Office was new, the system itself was ancient. The question of how to reform it had long been debated by engineers, lawyers and politicians. In the second quarter of the 19th century a national reform movement had developed, comprising many associations in London and the large manufacturing towns, similar to other pressure groups in this age of reform. Significant results were not achieved until the Patent Law Amendment Act of 1852. In context (though not to inventors) it was a minor reform among the many improvements of the time, in public health, policing, parliamentary representation and administration – so minor indeed that no general history in my experience has so far mentioned it.

The new office established procedures and founded publications that have stood the test of time, but it did more than meet these basic requirements of a patent system; it was characteristically Victorian or, more specifically, of the 1850s, the period that saw the founding of the South Kensington museums, the societies for popular education and the public libraries. Similar universalist aims and many of the people, professionals, politicians and public figures such as the Prince Consort also influenced the establishment of the Office, its Library and Patent Museum. The last was a now largely forgotten ancestor of the Science Museum.

For its first thirty years the Patent Office, or Great Seal Patent Office (as it continued to call itself) was under the authority of Commissioners appointed under the Act of 1852. This was an additional role for the holders of four traditional offices, those of Lord Chancellor, the Master of the Rolls, and the two Law Officers, the Attorney and Solicitor General. (The Law Officers of Scotland and Ireland were also nominally Commissioners.) These officials had traditionally been associated with the granting of letters patent, so the arrangement had a certain logic, false as it proved. The passing of control of the Office to the Board of Trade, the appointment of an executive head, the Comptroller, and of scientifically qualified staff under the Patents, Designs and Trade Marks Act of 1883 marked the end of a creative and eventful first phase. Parliament had laid down in some detail what the Office had to do but not how it was to do it. The new Act was the coming of age of patent law and administration.

There is a large and still fast growing literature on patents generally and on the history of the English system; the emphasis has been on law, the relation of patents to economics and the history of technology. In few areas of culture it seems to me, has so much discourse been deployed on such a narrow front. This study is not much about such things as patentability, claim drafting, the relation of invention to innovation, or present disputes about "patenting life". It is the story of an office during a period of change.

Abbreviations

BLSRIS SC	British Library, Science Reference and Information Service. Special Collections
CIPA Jnl	Chartered Institute of Patent Agents Journal
LQR	Law Quarterly Review
T&C	Technology and Culture
NST	Newcomen Society Transactions
RSA Jnl	Royal Society of Arts Journal
POESM	Patent Office Examining Staff Magazine
PRO	Public Record Office
SA Journal	Society of Arts Journal
SML	Science Museum Library
SMDC	Science Museum Documentation Centre

1 Some unoriginal history

For the reasons stated in the preceding, this section can only be the baldest summary of a great deal of scholarly work by others.

In his *Commentaries on the Laws of England*[1] published in the middle of the 18th century Sir William Blackstone provides an often quoted description of the physical embodiment of the King's grants, "whether of lands, honours, liberties, franchises or aught besides, contained in charters or letters patent, that is open letters, *literae patentes*, so called because they are not sealed up, with the Great Seal[2] pending at the bottom". Patents of invention were for long the most important of the "aught besides".

One can imagine a system of protecting the rights of inventors springing fully formed from a legislature, but that has not been the English way. Invention patents reflect a surprising amount of English history, from the obscure origins of the Great Seal, the token of royal authority, to the medieval Chancery, – both a civil "court of King's conscience" and royal secretariat – the conflict between Crown and Parliament in the late 16th and 17th century, and the increasing importance of invention from the industrial revolution to the present century.

United Kingdom invention patents originated in the grants conferring protection[3] and privileges on craftsmen and promoters of trade and processes which the Crown wanted to encourage. Many of the earliest were granted to aliens. Examples from the patent rolls in the public records have been studied and published by the Patent Office librarians E.W. Hulme, A. Gomme and others. In the 15th and 16th centuries[4] such grants were increasingly part of official policy for encouraging trade and invention. The principle of granting a temporary monopoly as an exception to general prohibition evolved in the late 16th and early 17th century as a product of widespread resentment[5] of the grants to individuals of monopolies in basic commodities and trades (for instance the hated monopoly in sweet wines that Sir Walter Raleigh among others enjoyed.) However, some historians have noted that monopolies did encourage economic activity and thus played an important part in early economic growth.

Elizabeth I's grants were attacked[6] by Parliament in late 1601 and first by proclamation via the Speaker and later in person she had to pronounce that her grants were for the "good and avail" of her subjects in general, and that she had been deceived. She deflected Parliament's challenge to her prerogative by promising that all such grants could be tested in the ordinary courts. In the "playing card" case (*Darcy v. Allin*, 1602)[7] the plaintiff sued for infringement of his monopoly in the import of cards. He lost because no invention was involved. The plaintiff's counsel then defined a principle in words that bear quoting yet again:

> Where any man by his own charge and industry or by his wit or invention doth bring any new trade into the Realm, or any engine tending to the furtherance of trade that never was used before; and that, for the good of the Realm; that in such cases the King may grant to him a monopoly patent for some reasonable time until the subjects may learn the same in consideration of the good he doth bring by his invention to the Commonwealth, otherwise not.

There was thus a well established common law recognition of invention before any statute.

Monopolies and the question of the extent of the prerogative figured largely in the increasingly assertive House of Commons in the later Parliaments of the reign of James I. In 1610 he had been compelled to publish a pamphlet, *A Declaration of His Maiesties Royall Pleasure in matter of Bountie* (reprinted in 1619).[8] Here the first of a list of illegalities is monopolies, but item 9 excepts "proiects of new invention" provided they are not otherwise illegal or harmful. In 1621 a Commons committee[9], in which the great champion of the common law Sir Edward Coke played a leading part, drew up a monopolies bill which was rejected by the Lords. After heated debate then and in the following Parliament, in May 1624 an *Act Concerning Monopolies and Dispensations with Penal Law*,[10] (21 Jac. I c.3) (colloquially called the Statute of Monopolies) was passed. It prohibited monopolies and annulled existing ones but recognised invention as a "Saving" i.e. exception in the case of:

> any letters patent and grants of privilege for the term of 14 years or under hereafter to be made of the sole making or working of any manner of new manufacture within this realm to the true and first

inventor and inventors ... as also they be not contrary to the law nor injurious to the state...

The term of 14 years for the duration of a patent which stood for many years is plausibly explained as the duration of two 7-year apprenticeships, enough for the transmission of a new trade.

"Manner of new manufacture" – the phrase has been an enduring touchstone for patentability, only challenged by late 20th century genetics.

The debates of 1623/4 were the Runnymede of United Kingdom patent history; the Statute, still in force, did not stop illegal monopolies such as played a part in the origins of the Civil War but it provided a working definition for the courts as patent cases became more prominent in the late 18th century. Those concerning the Adam brothers' stucco (*Liardet* v. *Johnson,* 1778), Arkwright's cotton machinery (*Rex* v. *Arkwright*, 1785) and James Watt's improvements to the steam engine (*Boulton and Watt* v. *Bull,* 1793) showed how patents could affect industrial progress and individual fortunes. They all depended on the adequacy of the specification.

Royal grants of privilege[11] always involved some "consideration" – a part of the profits, service to the Crown or benefit to the Commonwealth. The exact stages and rationale of the transition from other forms of consideration such as introducing a trade or craft, to the document that eventually discloses the invention "and the manner in which the same is to be performed" have been much debated. Evidently as machinery or complex process superseded crafts and trades as the subjects of patents, some written description comprehensible to those skilled in the art became essential. A number of early 17th century grants[12] contained the proviso that the patentee must supply the authorities with a "model" (drawing?) or description within a given time. Inventors were cagey of disclosure as they had no rights until the patent was sealed. In 1711 one inventor struck a bargain with the Law Officer that he would supply a specification within six months. By 1730 the grant contained wording making it void[13] if such a condition was not met. To many now, specification and patent are synonymous.

The obstacles to be overcome in the unreformed system[14], the procedure involving the Secretary of State, the Sovereign, the Law Officer, the

3

Signet, Privy Seal and Lord Chancellor's offices, the fees to many officials, are now a commonplace, the Chaffwax and All That. However ridiculous, they reflected the dignity of the constitution. Some practices originated in the safeguards necessary for the Great Seal in unsettled times, others were for the remuneration of unsalaried officials.

Examination by the Law Officers who lacked relevant knowledge was often unsatisfactory. There was uncertainty as to what a specification should contain[15]; Watt for instance feared the risks of the "frank and full" disclosure lacking which patents such as Arkwright's had fallen, and was forced into years of litigation. There was a lack of accessible information on other patents. Reform when achieved was limited.

Notes to Chapter I

1 Blackstone — *Commentaries on the Laws of England*, ed. R. M. Kerr, 1857, Vol.2. p.349.

2 the Great Seal — Maxwell-Lyte, H.C. *Historical Notes on the Use of the Great Seal*, London, HMSO, 1926.

3 the grants conferring protection — Hulme, Edward Wyndham, *The History of the Patent System under the Prerogative and at Common Law*, LQR, April, 1896, pp 1-14; *A Sequel*, LQR, January, 1900, pp 44-56; *On the History of the Patent Law in the 17th and 18th centuries*. LQR, July, 1902, pp. 280-288.

Gomme, Allan, *Patents of Invention, Origin and Growth of the Patent System in Britain*. The British Council; Longmans Green & Co., London, 1946 (1948) pp. 5-9. Also *Papers on Monopolies*, transcripts from the public records (unpublished papers) BLSRIS SC. Inlow, E. B., *The Patent Grant*, Baltimore, 1950, pp. 15-33.

4 In the 15th and 16th centuries — Fox, Harold G. *Monopolies and Patents: A Study of the History and Future of the Patent Monopoly*, Toronto UP, 1947. pp. 76-78. Gomme, A. as cited, p.12-13. His survey of Continental, especially Italian grants, pp. 6-9 is valuable.

5 resentment of the grants — Fox, as cited, pp. 76-78.

6 Elizabeth's grants were attacked — Gomme, as cited, pp. 13-14. The "Golden" speech is quoted in Neale, J. E. *Elizabeth I*, Pelican Biography, 1971, p. 389. Also in full in Jones, W. J. *The Elizabethan Court of Chancery*, Oxford, 1967, App. K.

7 *Darcy v. Allin*   Hayward, P. A., *Hayward's Patent Cases*, 1600–1883, Abingdon, 1987–88, reprints the contemporary records (pp. 2–8).

8 *Book of Bountie*   *A Declaration of His Maiesties Royall pleasure in what sort He thinketh fit to enlarge, or reserve Himself in matter of Bountie.* Imprinted at London by Robert Barker, … Anno 1610. BLSRIS SC, BG27, (71527); also Fox, H.G. as cited, pp. 96–98.

9 In 1621 a Commons Committee   Fox, as cited, pp. 102–112. For a more recent account, Kishlansky Mark, *A Monarchy Transformed*, Penguin History of Great Britain, v.6, 1997, p.100. Fox, as cited, pp. 113–126 .

10 Act Concerning Monopolies   Fox, as cited, pp 113–126. Dunlop J.H., *The Statute of Monopolies, Royal Assent 29th of May, 1624.*CIPA Jnl, April 1974 pp. 258–265. (Verbatim records).

11 Royal grants of privilege   Hulme, E.W., *On the Consideration of the Patent Grant, Past and Present*, LQR, 13, July, 1897, pp. 313–318. Davies, D. Seaborne, *The Early History of the Patent Specification*, LQR Jan, April, 1934, pp. 86–109; 260–274.

12 early 17th century grants   Gomme, A, *Patents of Invention*, pp. 25–35.

13 making it void   Gomme, A, *Patents of Invention*, pp. 33,34.

14 the unreformed system   Among many descriptions, Gomme, *Patents of Invention*, pp. 16–18; Davenport, Neil, *The United Kingdom Patent System*, Havant, 1979, pp. 15–17.

15 what a specification should contain   "The central criticism of the patent law by patentees was that it became next to impossible to specify an invention in a way that would satisfy the courts, and this because it had never been laid down exactly what a specification should do", Robinson, Eric, *James Watt and the law of Patents*, T. and C. 13.2 1972, pp. 115–139.

2 Approaches to reform

One of the earliest official edicts concerned with the examination of patents for inventions must be that of Queen Anne in 1713, who ordered The Royal Society[1] to scrutinise all new applications. In the 18th century grants for "patent" products were no more popular than the monopolies had been. Quack remedies were deplored in an anonymous pamphlet in 1760; the author proposed that The Royal Society of Physicians[2] should examine the many applications to patent medicines.

It is not surprising that in the last quarter of the 18th century, the makers of industrialisation such as James Watt and Richard Arkwright[3] were concerned with the damaging uncertainties of the system. Surviving papers in the Boulton and Watt archives, *Heads of a Bill* and *Thoughts upon Patents* among others reveal how Watt considered such questions as the nature of the specification, how disclosure could be made secure, expert assessment, improvement, additions and alterations. Watt gave evidence for Arkwright at the important trial in 1785 (*Rex* v. *Arkwright*) in which the latter's cotton carding patent was annulled. Josiah Wedgwood appears to have brokered a significant meeting between them after which Arkwright added some proposals of his own.

One of them was for the official publication of specifications.[4] Access to such records was a matter of concern at the time because of the likelihood of foreign piracy. A Committee of Patentees was formed in 1785[5] to press for restrictions. (The official obstacles complained of by so many 19th century reformers were evidently not insuperable.) Foreign piracy was far from the only kind, there was a home variety also.

In the early 19th century there was intensifying criticism from engineers, lawyers and other concerned professionals. Between 1820 and 1830 certain MPs[6], Charles Monk, J. C. Curwen and Sir John Wrottesley introduced measures that got no further than a reading. In 1827 the Commons[7] demanded statistics on invention patents. The request passed from the Secretary of State, Robert Peel, to the Chancellor, Lord Cottenham, and thence to the Keeper of the Rolls Chapel. There was an anxious exchange of memoranda between the Chancery clerks but the task proved too difficult.

The first official enquiry into patent law took place in 1829. A Commons Select Committee[8] on the Law Relative to Patents for Inventions heard evidence under the chairmanship of T. B. Lennard; it included the President of The Royal Society, Davies Gilbert. The witnesses included Marc Brunel, John Farey the civil and consulting engineer, W. H. Wyatt, editor of *The Repertory of Arts* and William Newton the patent agent. Despite producing a large volume of valuable evidence (including much from Farey on history, law and foreign patent systems) the Committee made no recommendations, the subject being "so intricate and important". It called for further enquiry in the next session, but none took place.

In 1833 yet another amendment bill[9] was introduced by Richard Godson, a barrister and author of a treatise on patents. It got as far as a reading in the Lords before vanishing from the record.

From the end of the 18th century, as inventions became more numerous there was evidently a "patent profession"[10]: lawyers specialising in patent cases, agents, consultants such as Farey, brokers (since patents were property) and venture capitalists. Farey himself was not a "smokestack" engineer but a man of scholarly inclination, not notably successful in business; Bennet Woodcroft was another. Some who practised as agents were in Government service; Harrison has identified four[11] who by 1846 "held positions in offices of state through which applications had to pass or in which specifications were enrolled".

The most famous, or notorious of these was Moses Poole.[12] He described himself as a clerk in the Attorney General's Patent Office and later, in 1849, as Clerk of Inventions – the title a sign of the times. He had inherited[13] the position from his father and combined it with a considerable practice as agent and "front" for many foreign patentees.[14] He testified that he found no difficulty in keeping the two roles separate. He was made redundant in 1852 and compensated[15] with £250 for life.

In line with the increase in inventions, published information on patents increased considerably in the first half of the 19th century, in the form of treatises, law reports and specifications in the technical press such as *The Mechanics' Magazine and Repertory of Arts*. They were also published as Record Office[16] reports.

One public measure that did reach the Statute Book was "Brougham's Act", *An Act to Amend the Law Touching Letters Patent for Inventions* (5,6 William IV c. 83) of 1835. It was intended to overcome the difficulties of patentees resulting from inadvertent infringement of existing patents. "Disclaimers and articles of alteration" could be lodged to amend a patent if found to be invalid. This Act introduced other minor improvements in the procedure for prolonging a patent and deterrents to frivolous actions for infringement.

By the early 1850s the reform movement[17] was nationwide, made up of various committees and associations; the name of one of the largest, the Art Protection Society[18] indicates that members were concerned with more than patent rights. Its membership included artists and craftsmen as well as engineers – Nasmyth, Whitworth, Rennie – and businessmen.

Many of them were also members of the Society of Arts. This London Society for the Encouragement of Arts, Manufactures and Commerce (not "Royal" until 1908) was nearly a century old and the senior – though not in years – of the many local improvement societies founded in the 18th century. After a period of shrinking membership[19] in the early 19th century its recovery in the 1840s reflected national progress and the growing importance of professionals and specialists. It combined the often not mutually exclusive qualities of fashion and competence. Its part in conceiving and realising the 1851 Exhibition[20] under its President the Prince Consort is well known. Its corporate influence and the contribution of individual members in the eventual realisation of patent reform were considerable.

In 1850 (?) the Council[21] of the Society printed a draft report for the consideration of its own Committee to Promote Legislative Recognition of the Rights of Inventors. This statement of the Society's *Principles of Jurisprudence* ... was a remarkable document for its time, containing powerful rhetoric against the Chancery system. It stressed that intellectual property was a right, not a privilege, a somewhat heretical view, and that to link it with monopoly was an error. The author's familiarity with the public records suggests that he was Henry Cole[22], who had formerly worked in the Record Office.

At this time the secretary of the special Committee and of the Society was George Grove[23], the engineer and musicologist (of the *Dictionary of*

Music). Charles Dickens[24] was a member. His satire on the traditional system in *Household Words* (1850) has become a cliché of patent history. It tells the story of an artisan like Daniel Doyce (in *Little Dorrit*) encountering the Circumlocution Office. When unpopular, the Patent Office was linked with this image for most of the century.

Two other Society members[25] are specially significant in the reform context, as James Harrison has shown, Thomas Webster and Bennet Woodcroft. Webster was a mathematician and scientist who became a barrister and writer on patent law. He had joined the Society in the 1840s and had much to do with its revival. He produced his own reform proposals and became to a great extent the draftsman of the Amendment Act. [26]

Woodcroft was an engineer, inventor and patent agent with a special interest in records, indexing and classification, in this particularly, a man of his time. In February, 1851,[27] he was associated with engineer friends from Birmingham and Manchester in delivering reform proposals to John Romilly the then Attorney General. Much more will be heard of him in the reformed Patent Office.

Notes to Chapter 2

1 The Royal Society — "in January (1713) the Fellows were informed that the Queen had given orders for them to scrutinise all new applications for patents of invention". In Smith, Allan, *Engines Moved by Fire and Water* NST, 66, 1994/5, pp. 1–25; note 85. From Royal Society, Journal Book C 13.1.1713.

2 The Royal Society of Physicians — Anon. *Short Reflections Upon Patents, Relating to the Abuses of that Noble Privilege ...* London, R. Griffith, 1760. BLSRIS SC BI30 (z) (61567).

3 James Watt and Richard Arkwright — Robinson, Eric, *James Watt and the Law of Patents,* T&C, 13, 2, April 1972, pp. 128–30.

4 Arkwright envisaged official publication — Robinson, as cited, p.129.

5 In 1785 a Committee — Robinson, p.131 from J. Watt to W. Matthews, 20.7.1875 (original in The Assay Library, Birmingham) Legislation in 1785 had forbidden export of certain machines and tools. p.130 f.n.48.

6 Between 1820 and
1830, certain MPs

J.C. Curwen and Charles Monk presented a bill on the
8th of February, 1821. 2nd reading postponed. (Hansard,
6.2.1821; 8.2.1821.) Motion to restrict access to
specifications proposed by Mr Wrottesley, 14.6.1821,
opposed by Mr Hume as "contrary to all liberal
practice." (Hansard).
J.C. Curwen, MP Carlisle, reformer and pamphleteer;
Charles Monk, MP Gloucester, President Assn of
Chambers of Commerce; Joseph Hume, radical MP
Aberdeen. Sir John Wrottesley (1771-1841) MP, Staffs,
1823-1832, S. Staffs, 1832-1837.

7 In 1827 the Commons

Robert Peel to the Lord Chancellor (Cottenham)
16.4.1827. MS in Lists and Letters Relating to the
Enrolment of Specifications, by H. W. Holden of the
Rolls Chapel. BL SRIS SC (46931).

8 A Commons Select
Committee

Report and Minutes, 12.6.1829, Parliamentary Papers,
1829.
Lennard, Thomas Barrett (1788-1856) MP, Maldon
Davies, Gilbert, (1767-1839) PRS, MP, Bodmin. Farey,
John, II, (1791-1851); History of the Steam Engine,
1827; Wyatt, Walter Henry, editor and proprietor,
Repertory of Arts.

9 another amendment
bill

Godson introduced proposals on 19:2:1833. He "asked
the indulgence of the House on the ground that the
subject was encompassed with many difficulties, and
there had not been any legislation... since James I
(Hansard). Leave for amendment bill given, 19.2.1833, In
committee, 9.7.1833. 3rd reading, 15.7.1833 Passed to
the Lords, 16.7.1833 (Hansard). Richard Godson, QC,
MP St Albans, mathematician reformer.

10 a patent profession

C. MacLeod, *Inventing the Industrial Revolution*,
Cambridge, 1988; James Harrison, *Some Patent
Practitioners Associated with the Society of Arts*, c.1790-1840,
RSA Journal, July, 1982, pp. 494-498; 589-594.

11 Harrison has
identified four

As cited, RSA Jnl, 1982, p.496.

12 Moses Poole

Select Committee on the Law Relative to Patents for
Inventions, Report, 1829. Evidence, p.82. Committee on
the Signet and Privy Seal Offices 1849. Minutes, p.52-.

13 He had inherited

MS correspondence in Francis Poole, Casebook from
1786, justifying his position. BLSRIS SC, BJ00 (54889).
The book was saved and donated to POL by R.B.
Prosser.

14 many foreign patentees   Patent Office. Alphabetical Index of Patentees, 1617–1852 passim.

15 redundant in 1852 and compensated   Commissioners of Patents, Annual Reports, Compensations figures, 1854–

16 Record Office   Report of the Deputy Keeper (Rolls Chapel Repts) 6th, 1845–

17 the reform movement   Harding, *Patent Office Centenary*, 1953, pp.5-7; many provincial press notices in scrapbook, Patent Law. BLSRIS SC, BJ00p (267).

18 Art Protection Society   Draft prospectus (printed) BLSRIS SC, Scrapbook as cited, item 5.
Members, James Nasmyth (1808-1890) ironfounder, industrialist, inventor. His friendship with Woodcroft is well documented. George Rennie, eldest son of John (1761-1821) mechanical engineer; Joseph Whitworth, (1803-1887) toolmaker.

19 shrinking membership   J. Harrison, *RSA Journal*, 1982, p.672.

20 its part in... the 1851 Exhibition   H. T. Wood, *A History of the Royal Society of Arts*, Murray, 1913, pp. 404-415.

21 the Council printed a draft Report   *On the Principles of Jurisprudence which should regulate the recognition of the rights of inventors*. BLSRIS SC Patent reform scrapbook, BJt (237) item 19.

22 Henry Cole   (1808-1822) Chairman of Council, SA, 1850. First Director, South Kensington Museum.

23 George Grove   (1820-1900) knighted, 1882. Secretary, SA, 1850-1852. Secretary, Crystal Palace Company. Cole's and Grove's links with the Patent Office, see Ch.13.

24 Charles Dickens   *Household Words*, no 30, Saturday, Oct.19 1850, pp.73-75. *Little Dorrit*, Bk I, Ch. 10, pp.113-122; Ch.23, pp.253-269; Bk II, Ch.22, pp.638-641. (Everyman edn. Dent, 1969.)

25 Two other Society members   Harrison, as cited, RSA Jnl, 1982, pp.671-2.

26 Webster became in effect   House of Commons, Select Committee on Letters Patent, Report and Minutes, 20.7.1871, Webster, Q.537.

27 In February 1851 he was associated   *The Manchester Guardian*, 17.2.1851, SRIS, scrapbook, Patent reform, as cited.

3 The Patent Law Amendment Act, July 1852

In 1851 Lord John Russell's administration at last took firm steps toward reform. The Exhibition brought about an unprecedented awareness of the importance of manufactures and especially of British manufactures. Temporary protection for not yet patented inventions was provided[1] by an Act passed a few weeks before it opened in May, using the registration machinery of an earlier Designs Act administered by the Board of Trade. The showing or demonstration of an invention would not prejudice later application for a patent.

Reform did not come easily; the number of Bills[2], at least nine, testified to the difficulties of framing a new and very specialised system and a new office. The first bill was introduced by Lord Brougham, the former reforming Chancellor who had a continuing interest in such matters. This was followed by a Government Bill introduced by Lord Granville. Both were submitted to a House of Lords select committee[3] which heard evidence from April to June, 1851. Chaired by Granville, it included the 3rd Earl of Rosse the astronomer; John Campbell the biographer of lawyers; and Lord Broughton who, as John Cam Hobhouse, had been Byron's friend. The new generation of witnesses included Cole, Webster and Woodcroft. Most agreed on the urgent need of reform, differing only on the extent of departure from the old system and on the important question of expert examination of specifications. The patent agent William Carpmael was one of the few in favour of the status quo – agents had a vested interest in it. I. K. Brunel was opposed[4] to patents on principle. Woodcroft demonstrated[5] his indexing system and was eloquent in the cause of inventors generally. Webster became in effect a committee member and drafted a new bill drawing on Brougham's and Granville's, which the committee presented in the briefest possible report, but accompanied by a massive blue book of evidence.

After many revisions in both Houses, The Patent Law Amendment Act, was passed in July, 1852[6], by a different Government from the one under which it had been prepared. In February, Russell's administration had been replaced[7] by Lord Derby's, a result of Palmerston's "tit for tat with Johnny Russell" – patent reform was a non-party matter.

The lengthy Act at last made possible though it did not ordain a single office for invention patents under newly created Commissioners of Patents, in fact the incumbents of the offices of Lord Chancellor, Master of the Rolls and the six Law Officers for England, Scotland and Ireland. There would be a single patent for the United Kingdom thus abolishing Scottish and Irish grants. The Law Officers for Scotland and Ireland thus had no real function except to receive published specifications. They and their clerks were amply compensated for years to come for loss of fees as were those of the almost redundant Patent Bill office (Compensations totalled £6,000 in 1853, some £300,000 in modern terms).

Other important clauses ordained the publication of notices of applications and the lodging of either a provisional or a complete specification. (Under the old law some patentees had offered provisional specifications.) Some saw the clause concerning the examination of specifications as a missed opportunity. Thomas Webster had wanted it taken out of the hands of the Law Officers except for a preliminary check for legality. It had originally read "it shall be lawful for the Commissioners from time to time to appoint a person or persons as examiner or examiners" and "the provisional specification shall be referred by the Law Officers ... to one or more of the examiners".

Giving evidence in 1871[8] he ruefully recalled how this was amended in the Commons; the Act merely empowered the Law Officer "to call to his aid such scientific or other persons as he thinks fit". Earlier in his manual on the Act[9], he had described how his measure was weakened and there was no time for further consideration in the Lords. "This duty of preliminary examination spoken to by almost every witness as of paramount importance, the committee of the House of Commons thought fit to impose upon the Law Officers..." and he predicted grievous disappointment for patentees.

Harding, a former examiner, called the 1851 proceedings[10] "a good example of optimistic Victorian attempts to legislate in the public interest on a high moral plane and of failure to distinguish between the ideal and the possible". In the matter of examiners, Parliament had a fair grasp of the possible; it was not clear how they were to be found; there were no suitable civil servants or, at the time, organised records for them to use.

Excessive optimism was certainly apparent in the clauses concerning records and publication (XXX, XXXI, and XXXII) which, in addition to calling for publication of indexes to all patents "heretofore and hereafter", also required removal of records from the three Chancery repositories to the new Office. As described below (Ch.6) publication of complete specifications was accomplished without removal, as well as of Woodcroft's and subsequent indexes. The high-minded clause calling for distribution of publications to the new public libraries was more than generously effected.

For the first time the Act required a Register of Patents, recording all grants in chronological sequence, with later additions and amendments, likewise a Register of Proprietors, to enter all vicissitudes of ownership. The precise procedure for obtaining a patent of invention was on the statute book for the first time as a result of the Act.

It was evolutionary rather than revolutionary. Patentees, as in Dickens' *Tale* had been "chaffed and waxed sufficient" but the initial humble petition to the Sovereign, the large parchment Law Officer's warrant and even larger grant with many of their traditional verbal forms (though engrossed by lithography) and – at least until the 1870s – the ceremonial of the Great Seal, remained. Property in invention, if to all intents a right, was still attired as a privilege.

Not everyone welcomed the Act; *The Mechanics' Magazine*[11], one of the few such journals at the time denounced the changes at first. It compared the paperwork under the old and new systems, noting that some formalities had already been done away with by the recent abolition of the Signet Office in 1851. (The Privy Seal Office survived until the 1880s but after the Act its delays were no longer a trial to inventors.) "The interests of the inventor and rightly understood of the public are sacrificed to the innovating rage of a set of state tinkers", it fumed. The many improvements under the Act were ignored. This eccentric reaction was probably the retiring view of the editor, J.C. Robertson ("Sholto Percy", 1788-1852) founder of the magazine who did not live long enough to see the working of the Act. His successor soon disowned such a view.

Notes to Chapter 3

1 Temporary protection was provided   Designs Act, Amended, 14 Vict., c.8.

2 the number of Bills   BLSRIS SC Collection of patent bills BJ00t.

3 Lords select committee   Select Committee of the House of Lords appointed to consider the bill ... Report and Minutes, 1.7.1851. BLSRIS SC BJ00t (289).

4 I.K. Brunel was opposed   Report, as cited, Minutes, 22nd May Q, 1767-1837.

5 Woodcroft demonstrated   Minutes, 20th May, Q 1558-1686.

6 Patent Law Amendment Act   15,16 Vict. c.83.

7 Russell's administration had been replaced   Jenkins, Roy (Lord Jenkins of Hillhead) *Gladstone*, Macmillan, 1995, ch.9 p. 138.

8 Webster, giving evidence in 1871   Select Committee on Letters Patent, Report and Minutes, 20.7.1871, Q.549-561. BLSRIS SC, BJt (15792).

9 his manual on the Act   Webster, T. *The New Patent Law*, F. Elsworth, London, 1853 p. 46.

10 Harding... called the 1851 proceedings   *Patent Office Centenary*, 1952, pp. 9.10.

11 *The Mechanics' Magazine*   1 May, 1852, 56, p.387.

4 A commodious office?

The Patent Office opened for business[1] on October lst, 1852. For its first three months it was in so far unidentified premises[2] for which a rent of £25 was paid. This may have been in Quality Court, off Chancery Lane, on the south side of the eventual site; there were press references to it after the move.

Three months later, on December 29th, it moved to the partly vacant offices of The Masters in Ordinary in Chancery, at 25 Southampton Buildings, Holborn. The "Buildings" are in fact a narrow street, an L–shaped backwater linking High Holborn to Chancery Lane, with access to Staple Inn to the east. One staff member[3] noted at the time that he thought this address would be temporary, as no lease was taken.

The first set of Commissioners' Rules to be published had optimistically stated, "Whereas a commodious office is forthwith to be provided by the Crown as the Great Seal Patent Office...".[4] (In this instance, "forthwith" was to mean nearly 50 years.) The present offices had been built[5] as a result of late 18th century legislation allowing the High Court of Chancery to invest suitors money, using the interest for various purposes, including building new offices for the Masters, and for the Secretaries of Bankrupts and Lunatics. The first part was built by 1797.[6]

That they were available was a result of the same reforming climate that brought about a new Patent Office. The popular view of Chancery apparent in Dickens' *Bleak House* and *Little Dorrit*[7] is evident in a contemporary description of the Masters:

> ...secluded in the recesses of their dark chambers, exempt from the control or inspection of the judges, relieved from the competition of the bar, independent of the opinion of solicitors and their proceedings totally unknown to the public; acquiring no credit by diligence or ability, incurring neither loss nor censure by indolence or inattention, with nothing to hope and nothing to fear.

By legislation drafted during Lord Truro's chancellorship (July 1850 – February 1852) and passed a few weeks before the Patent Law Amendment Act, the jurisdiction of the twelve Masters was abolished and a modern system of judges in chambers established. The Masters were retired on full salary for life[8], as was the custom with redundant senior posts.

Prospective patentees perhaps noticed that the office intended to remove some of Chancery's delays now shared a building that had been the embodiment of them. One authority has described the frontage[9] of the Master's office as "palladian" on the evidence of 19th century photographs. They show a gloomy facade with massive rusticated round-arched windows above a basement, with an upper floor behind a screen of Roman Doric columns. Entrance steps led to a narrow corridor lit by two cupolas[10] and leading to the Quality Court frontage and the Bankruptcy and Lunacy offices.

When the old offices were being demolished in 1902, *The Builder* invited its readers[11] to see "what we believe is the last work in London by Sir William Chambers that was completed during his lifetime":

> It forms the Southern facade – a classic order with rusticated ground floor and an angle pediment in Portland stone of the offices originally built for the then Masters in Chancery..."

John Harris, an expert on Chambers[12] has suggested that an attribution to him is unlikely and that he would have passed the commission to an assistant such as John Yenn.

Nineteenth century photographs of the exterior are misleading as to the accommodation in 1852. A ground plan of 1857 shows that a large extension had been built[13] in an east by south direction, with many small rooms around a central corridor. It had been described some years before the Patent Office moved in:

> Each set contains a room[14] about twenty feet square lighted by one window in which the Master sits; two smaller rooms each of them passages to his room occupied by his two clerks, one lighted by half a window, the other dark.

The central corridor was to be part of the first library.

In the heart of legal London the site has its advantages and still has many patent agents as neighbours. "The only desirable thing[15] about the English office is its situation" commented *The Engineer* in 1857, comparing it with the US Patent Office in Washington, adding (ironically?) "it is also surrounded by the delightful atmosphere of the Courts of Chancery". It was, as it still is, a district of lawyers, but then also of booksellers, patent agents, instrument and map sellers, and law stationers.

At first the Patent Office occupied only the ground floor[16], the upper was still used by Chancery registrars. Chancery was the landlord, the rent, £355 for the first year, went to the Suitors Fee Fund.

It was an appropriate time for the establishment of an office with an increasingly important role in fostering invention. The worst stresses of the 1840s – "the hungry forties" – had been eased and the 1851 Exhibition had been a triumphant success. Just down the road however, public executions still took place outside Newgate, and other vestiges of the 18th century persisted in the Government service.

The informal arrangement of the Office – as it was nowhere laid down – was into a Patent Division under Leonard Edmunds (who kept the post he had held since 1833 of Clerk of the Patents) and a Specification Division under Bennet Woodcroft, an arrangement reflecting the form of a patent, the grant to the inventor and the technical part, the specification. Edmunds was also given a new title of Clerk of the Commissioners of Patents and kept the two offices[17] he held in the House of Lords, of Reading Clerk and Clerk of Outdoor Committees. He enjoyed a salary of £400 as Clerk of the Patents and £600 as Clerk of the Commissioners, a total, from the Patent Office alone, exactly equal to Woodcroft's £1,000 as Superintendent of Specifications.

They were men of contrasting backgrounds and personalities: Woodcroft[18] from the new manufacturing class and a region noted for liberalism, free trade and free knowledge. He was born near Stockport in Lancashire in 1803, the son of John Woodcroft, a dyer and velvet finisher whose family had long standing links with Sheffield where they owned property. After shop-floor training in textiles (he "worked at the loom" wrote his obituarist) he went into partnership with his father. This was not a success and he set up on his own as an inventor and consultant. He took out patents for improvements in textile machinery and textile printing, and for marine propellers, one of which was fitted with success to Brunel's *SS Great Britain*. He moved to London and continued practice as a patent agent, becoming involved, as noted above, with the Society of Arts. For a short and unsatisfactory period he was Professor of Machinery at University College. Four years before joining the Patent Office he had published *A Sketch of the Origin, and progress of Steam Navigation*, and this interest in the history and archives of technology was sometimes carried to near eccentric lengths. Shortly before taking up his appointment he had edited another lavishly produced historical work, a translation of the classical *Pneumatics*, of Hero of Alexandria, stylishly printed by Whittingham at Took's Court and dedicated to Prince Albert (1851).

A report[19] of his appointment in *The Manchester Guardian* exemplified the usually good press he received throughout his career, and throws some light on the public attitude to government service at the time:

> Professor Bennet Woodcroft – One of the most recent appointments made by the late ministry will, we think, give universal satisfaction, at all events we are sure that his very numerous friends in Manchester and Lancashire generally, as well as those of more recent date in the Metropolis will rejoice to learn that Professor Bennet Woodcroft – best known to the scientific world perhaps by his patent screw propeller for marine and river steamers – has received in a way which reflects honour on all parties concerned a responsible and permanent appointment – one for life indeed in a department where his intimate and extensive knowledge and practical acquaintance with its details pre-eminently qualify him.

Edmunds' background[20] was very different; the two could have been chosen to exemplify the social changes of the first half of the 19th century. His father had been in the political service of the gentry in rural Westmoreland, and his career so far was a product of the patronage system, under which office was still regarded as a form of property and duties sometimes done by deputy. Born c. 1802 he was the son of John Edmunds of Ambleside who had been election agent to Henry Peter Brougham, lawyer, mathematician and Edinburgh reviewer, later a reforming Chancellor. Edmunds senior had been killed in a road accident while canvassing during the election of 1826. Brougham felt obliged to help the family and arranged for Leonard to enter the office of his own solicitors in Lincoln's Inn.

Before his present posts in the Lords, Edmunds had held several Chancery offices through the Brougham influence. He was made Clerk of the Patents in 1833. Unmarried, he boarded at Lord Brougham's London house[21], and claimed to have been his confidential – and unpaid – secretary. With his legal training and Chancery background, Edmunds was experienced in the formalities of traditional government service.

With Thomas Ruscoe his chief clerk of long standing and five other clerks, Edmunds' division would be responsible for all the non-technical documentation, from the initial petition to the sealing of the grant. As Clerk of the Patents he remained responsible for the documentation of non-invention patents which was unchanged by the reforms, patents of appointment to state offices and charters to corporate bodies. Patents of nobility remained under the Crown Office. (The fact that non-invention patents[22] were partly paid for in fees, while patents of invention were soon to be paid for in revenue stamps, has some bearing on the "Edmunds affair" of 1864/5.) Edmunds considered himself with some justification as office manager, responsible for accounts and supplies.

As Superintendent of Specifications, Woodcroft was to be responsible for putting into practice many of the innovations under the Act, the passing and publishing of specifications, indexing and other publications which were soon extensive. His division had an initial staff of only two, but it soon grew more rapidly than Edmunds'. Neither official was young; Woodcroft was in his 47th year and Edmunds perhaps a year older.

The first historian of the Office has called this organisation under the Commissioners "extraordinary". They were all holders of important legal offices, three of them changing with each administration. In Woodcroft's obituary (1879) his friend and colleague R.B. Prosser referred to the problems of a system of concurrent jurisdiction. In view of the friction which led to the Edmunds "scandal" of 1864/5, and the derogatory view of him generally presented, such evidence as there is of the initial setting up of the Office is of interest. According to Edmunds' own account[23], the then Chancellor, Lord St Leonards[24] asked him to take charge of and organise the Office. Edmunds and his clerks were officially appointed on the day the Office opened, October 1st. His account suggests a

Chancellor less than enthusiastic:

> Before I left town in 1852 I had communicated verbally with the Lord Chancellor, and called his attention to the necessity of making regulations for the purpose of bringing the Act into operation. He desired me to come back to town in September; he said he would not begin the business before. I saw him frequently at Boyle Farm [His residence at Thames Ditton]. He said this was a pretty business; it seemed intended to create a good many offices and jobs, but that shouldn't be; there must be one head to supervise everything.

Evidently the Victorian culture of the sacrosanct Long Vacation (for the professional classes) played a part in office history.

Woodcroft's letter of appointment[25] was as late as December 6th, 1852, the post being decided at a Commissioners meeting in November. As late as the previous August he was offering in a printed circular[26] to supply references from his indexes at a shilling a time. Was he still in private business?

He claimed that he had been appointed Assistant to the Commissioners but in the first annual report from the Office this was changed to Superintendent of Specifications, by Edmunds, he alleged. He remembered this slight[27] for years.

Woodcroft has rightly become the hero of Patent Office history, nevertheless the facts suggest that eventual disgrace has obscured the modicum of credit Edmunds deserves for his part in its establishment and early operation.

Notes to Chapter 4

1 The Patent Office opened for business   Commissioners of Patents, *Annual Report*, 1852-3 (1853) p.l.

2 unidentified premises   Annual Report, as cited, Current and Incidental Expenses, p.20.

3 one staff member noted   Woodcroft, excerpt from Minute Book 29.12.1852. BLSRIS SC Woodcroft Collection.

4 Whereas a commodious Office   Commissioners of Patents, First set of Rules, 1.10.1852 p.2. SRIS SC, BJ00f L.

5 the Offices had been built   Caswell, Brian, POESM no 183, Nov. 1975, p.5. (*History of the Patent Office site.*)

6 built by 1797   Caswell, as cited, p.6.

7 description of the Masters   Campbell, John, *Lives of the Lord Chancellors*, 1839–1855, vol 2, p.451, Lord Truro, quoting Pemberton-Leigh, Thomas, in Parliament in 1840.

8 full salary for life   as granted to William Brougham, brother and heir to Lord Brougham. See Ch.8.

9 One authority has described the frontage   Tyack, Geoffrey, *Sir James Pennethorne, and the Making of Victorian London*. CUP 1992. p. 275.

10 lit by two cupolas   Harding, *Patent Office Centenary*, p.35.

11 *The Builder* invited its readers   18. 1.1902.

12 an expert on Chambers   John Harris, personal communication. 27.6.1991.

13 a large extension had been built   Caswell, as cited, p. 9.

14 set contains a room   Caswell, p.8, from an unspecified pamphlet of 1841.

15 only desirable thing   *The Engineer*, 31.7.1857

16 occupied only the ground floor   Harding, as cited, p.35.

17 Edmunds kept the two offices   Sainty, John (Sir John) *The Edmunds Case and the House of Lords*. CIPA Jnl, Nov. 1983. Also printed in *Festschrift for Maurice Bond*, for private circulation.

18 Woodcroft   A useful beginning is his obituary, in *The Engineer*, 47, 14.2.1879, p.118 by R. B. Prosser.

19 A report of his appointment   reprinted in *The Mechanics' Magazine*, 2.1.1853, p.10.

20 Edmunds' background   Sainty, CIPA Jnl, as cited.

21 boarded at Lord Brougham's London house   Sainty, as cited, f.n.7.

22 non-invention patents   these for which fees were paid were investigated in detail as part of the Hindmarch-Greenwood enquiry, 1864/5 and accounts published in *Papers Relating to the Patent Office*. See Ch.8, *The Edmunds Affair*.

23 Edmunds' account suggests   *Papers Relating to the Patent Office*, Minutes, 2.6.1864, p.82.

24 Lord St Leonards   Edward Burtenshaw Sugden (1781–1875).

25 Woodcroft's letter of appointment   Select Committee on the Patent Office, Library and Museum. Report, 19.7.1864, Minutes, Woodcroft, Q.86.

26 a printed circular   headed The Patent Law Amendment Act datelined 3 Furnival's Inn, Aug. 1852. BLSRIS SC, *Patent Law* scrapbook, item 20. BJ00p (237).

27 He remembered this slight   Library and Museum Report, 1864 as cited, Minutes, Woodcroft, Q.89–91.

5 Open for business

Whether or not Woodcroft had taken up his post, the Office immediately became busy. (He very probably had, as the earliest printed specifications have illustrations lithographed "R.Prosser" i.e. his friend Richard Prosser senior.) Some 147 + applications[1] were received at the temporary office on the first day, a figure which fell to a mere 48 on the second. The simpler and cheaper patent had been eagerly anticipated. There were signs of inadequate preparation: some of the procedures and wording of the principal documents had been prescribed in a Schedule to the Act but I have found no evidence that printed forms were ready for applicants at this stage. A few journals of interest to inventors such as *The Mechanics' Magazine* published the Act in full. Civil servants with the experience to introduce complex public measures of the kind we associate with food rationing or welfare hardly existed.

The Office did issue Rules[2], under the Commissioners' authority, stating the dimensions of documents, opening hours and charges. The number of issues also indicates some lack of preparation. The earliest, issued before the opening, appeared only in the journals and was cancelled a fortnight later by a separate notice. Some were signed by the Chancellor, some by the Master of the Rolls Sir John Romilly (1802-1874), some by the Law Officers of this short-lived administration Sir Frederick Thesiger (1794-1878) and Sir Fitzroy Kelly (1796-1880) and some by all four. An important rule such as that the application should be for one invention only, did not appear until 1853. The lack of continuity in such an arrangement is emphasized by the fact that before the Office had moved into the Masters offices on the 29th of December 1852, three of the Commissioners were replaced; Lord Cranworth (Robert Monsey Rolfe, 1790-1868) became Chancellor, Sir Alexander Cockburn (1802-1880) Attorney General, and Sir Richard Bethell (1800-1873) Solicitor General, in Lord Aberdeen's Government.

Much remains unclear about these early days as the more newsy engineering journals did not yet exist. Nevertheless by the following January the stream of published specifications had begun as required by the Act. By 1854[3] the Office had certainly published its own text of the Act, with the Rules and a set of blank forms for the Petition, Provisional

Specification and Declaration. Those "still unacquainted with the mode of proceeding", were directed to solicitors or patent agents. By 1859 a form was available to reply to postal enquiries including much other information about the Commissioners' publications, by then extensive.

Though simpler than the old system and run almost wholly from one office, patenting was still elaborate and still resembled the traditional Chancery procedure in which each document, when approved, was filed as the warrant for the next one.

The applicant first chose a title for the invention beginning e.g. "improvements in…". Exponents of the new law such as Webster stressed the importance of not claiming too much, which might invalidate the patent in the courts. He then had to prepare three documents[4], a Petition to the Sovereign, humbly requesting the grant of letters patent, a Provisional Specification briefly describing "the nature of the said invention" to which drawings of a specified size could be added, and the Declaration, an affidavit stating that the invention was new and was the inventor's own. His signature had to be witnessed by a JP or Master Extraordinary in Chancery. On the principle that the state should gain some consideration in exchange for the grant the Declaration also stated that the invention would prove "of great public benefit". The Petition was stamped[5] at £5, the first payment. A full specification also stamped at £5 could be submitted instead of a provisional one.

The three documents were presented at the public counter, for this purpose presumably manned by Edmunds' staff, were dated, numbered, and a Certificate of Record given. The Petition was endorsed by the Clerk of the Commissioners (Edmunds) on behalf of the Crown (an important change replacing the personal involvement of the Secretary of State and Sovereign). The documents were then referred to one of the Law Officers, the Attorney and Solicitor General, it is said, taking them alternately as the fees, though halved soon[6] from the initial 4 guineas, totalled very large sums. The Officer's function was, in theory, to decide whether the invention was patentable and consistent with the title; in Webster's words whether it showed any "inconsistency, vagueness or want of distinctiveness".

The Law Officers dealt with applications in chambers, the documents, according to one anecdote, being brought by cab[7], though this is

25

contradicted by a statement by Edmunds[8] that cabs could be hired only when taking patents for sealing.

The papers were returned to or, more probably, collected by the Patent Office with the Law Officer's Certificate of Allowance of Provisional Protection. From the date this was filed the invention was protected and could be used and publicised, an important reform. A notice of the grant of protection was published in *The London Gazette* giving the name of the patentee and title and from 1854 in *The Patent Journal*.

The applicant next gave Notice of Intention to Proceed on a document carrying a £5 stamp, the second payment. No form of words was given in the Schedule of the Act but an accepted form was soon in use. This notice was also published. The application could now be opposed, by means of a Notice of Particulars of Objection stamped at £2. If it was, both parties were summoned to a hearing before the Law Officer, each paying £2 12s 6d to the latter and a modest sum to his clerk. Law Officer hearings were unpopular with patent reformers, both before and after the 1852 Act. The Officer could award costs against the unsuccessful opposer.

The provisional or complete specification was again referred to the Law Officer who issued his Warrant[9] to the Chancellor for the patent to be granted. For many years after the Act this was an impressive parchment but certainly in later examples with the engrossment in facsimile rather than by hand. (With such large numbers of documents, the Office took advantage of such reprography as was available, e.g. lithography.) The warrant "in humble obedience to Her Majesty's command" advised the Chancellor that the patent could be granted but made clear that it was "entirely at the hazard of the said petitioner whether the said invention was new or would have the desired success". The patentee had a right to defend his invention but was otherwise on his own. The warrant was stamped at £5 – and looked well worth it. Signed by the Law Officer and Chancellor, it was filed at the Office. Renewal payments at 3 and 7 years were endorsed on it, with the Clerk of the Commissioners signature and the Office seal.

The warrant was nevertheless modest compared with the grant which was then made out in the Patent Division. It was a large parchment some 2 ft wide with an elaborate heading and border. (The first Office accounts record "Paid for copperplate engraving for ornamental border for patents, for transferring the designs to lithographic stones and for the stones, £18.") A grant for 1865[10] shows Britannia and Justice, flanking the royal arms, with a border of oak leaves and ropes sheltering *putti*. The wording is, as with the warrants, in facsimile MS. Pre-reform grants usually had a portrait of the King or Queen. These reflections of the dignity of the constitution continued until 1878 when they were replaced by plainer documents and token seal.

Resembling a royal proclamation, beginning "To all to whom these presents may come" and in its archaic diction, the post-reform patent differed little from those of earlier centuries. It was still sealed by attaching an impression of the Great Seal to the lower edge by a coloured cord. The seal was protected by a japanned tin box, slotted for the cord to pass through. The first 15 months' accounts, under "Current and incidental expenses" record "Paid the Sealer of the Court of Chancery for wax expended upon 2,388 impressions…£179.9s 6d with similar figures for tin boxes".[11] This extravagant use of the Great Seal was surely a new phenomenon in English history. The only early ground plan of the Office shows a Sealer's room.

Edmunds recorded[12] that "the sealing of the patents is ordinarily appointed two days in the week, wherever the Lord Chancellor may be, the House of Lords or his residence. Twenty to twenty five are conveyed for sealing in cabs". If the Chancellor was out of town in the long vacation – its duration makes present-day lawyers seem quite hard worked – the patents were taken to him by messenger, and special payments were made[13] "for obtaining the seals to patents during the vacation". Presumably the sealer went too.

Full specifications, if not submitted instead of the provisional, had to be lodged within six months of the date of provisional protection. As with other documents their form was prescribed. At first, large parchments were required as they had been pre-1852, but this was changed to allow paper. Parchment, cloth or paper could be used for drawings. The specification was stamped at £5, the fifth payment.

Obviously many inventors had delayed applying until the new and cheaper patent was available. What of the others? There was a curious transition period during 1852-3. Specifications of several patents granted before the Act were not submitted until 1853 when it was in force. They were endorsed in the traditional way, with the statement that "on this day ... did appear before our Sovereign Lady the Queen in Her Chancery" and were signed by the Chancery clerk. This picturesque formula did not survive the new Act. These few transitional patents were enrolled in the traditional way, but were also printed like the new law patents, being sent to the back of the queue, some not appearing for several years.

This period evidently confused the Record Office. Its manuscript indexes do not distinguish[14] between the new law and old law patents, and for a time continued to enter the printed ones. Eventually the clerks realised that the Patent Office had taken over part of their job.

Inevitably there were some early changes in the working of the complex Amendment Act, notably in the method of payment for a patent. Traditionally payment had been made[15] by a combination of the notorious fees and revenue stamp duty on the documents. Certain stages, such as the grant, required a fee and stamp duty. Under the Amendment Act the only stage paid for by a stamp duty alone was the Law Officer's warrant. Most were paid as before by fees, and the rest by stamp duties and fees. An important change under the Act, linked to the introduction of the cheaper patent, required the renewal of a patent by further payments at the end of three and seven years, the latter being by far the largest single payment. (Renewal is an index of the success of an invention – most of the flood of new patents after 1852 lapsed at the end of three years.)

Under the Act these were paid by a £40 fee and £10 stamp after three years and a final £80 fee and £20 stamp. In February 1853 an Act[16] "to substitute Stamp Duties for fees on passing letters patent for inventions" was passed. This ended at last the practice of separate fees. The three and seven year renewals were now paid by £50 and £100 stamps. Returns of fees vanished from the published accounts. Puzzlingly, Revenue Stamp Duties and Fee Stamp Duties were listed on opposite sides of the accounts, the former as a Payment. The Act required the Stamp Office to prepare suitable adhesive stamps, which were also to be used as receipts on sales of documents and publications.

The Inland Revenue was gratified[17] enough to include the Patent Office in the departments "collecting their duties and fees with the safety and economy afforded by…stamps". Stamps eliminated separate receipts and the accumulation of large sums to be paid in to the Consolidated Fund. The Patent Office now bought stamps at Somerset House with money paid in by applicants as required. Small denomination adhesive stamps could be taken to the Office but for the more expensive stamps the stamping was probably done at the Stamp Office on paper supplied there or from law stationers such as Sackett and Ruscoe. (Edmunds' clerk Thomas Ruscoe later described his visits to the Stamp Office[18].) These "blue deed" stamps[19] consist of a rectangle of special paper, blue or otherwise coloured measuring 2 x 1 1/2 in., secured to the document by a strip of soft tin passed through two slits in the coloured paper and the document and bent over at the back. The ends were covered by a glued paper label carrying the royal monogram. The whole sandwich was then diestamped with the denomination. This elaborate construction was to prevent re-use. Such stamps are a conspicuous feature of pre-modern patent (and of course other) documents. The practice of buying stamps at the Stamp Office was to have dire consequences for Edmunds and his chief clerk.

This 1853 Act re stamps also allowed the purchase for the nation of Woodcroft's indexes to the pre-1852 patents, for £1,000.

The Law Officers' fee for passing provisional or complete specifications, left open in the Amendment Act, had been set at 4 guineas at a Commissioners' meeting in December 1852. In May, 1853 the two senior commissioners, Lord Cranworth and Sir John Romilly halved the scale of fees[20] on the grounds that the original fees "will in the aggregate amount to a much larger sum than is reasonable". Payments to the law officers were indeed more than was reasonable and became notorious when the first accounts were published. During the first three months of operation Frederick Thesiger and Fitzroy Kelly were each paid £2,500, and the total fees to the law officers and their clerks by the end of 1853 came to over £21,000. The Act allowed for compensation for loss of emoluments, and well into the 1870s large sums continued to be paid to the Scottish and Irish law officers and their staffs. In an age of Treasury tight-fistedness, officials, as always, protected their own species. Edmunds plausibly claimed[21] that he had achieved the fee reduction. He was a cost conscious official and deserves some posthumous credit for the published accounts that tell the story however suspect some of them may be, in view of later events.

Much of the work of the Specification Division consisted of processing specifications for publication. The applicant's text was examined and the title amended if necessary. The clerks styled themselves "examiners"[22] long before there were any official examiners.(In 1855 the small staff[23] were given a salary increase on the grounds that they were experienced mechanical draughtsmen.) A manuscript copy was made for the printers. The work of both divisions must have involved vast amounts of pen-pushing but much of this was done by stationer's writers paid piecework rates. Soon after the Office opened there were almost as many writers as salaried clerks in the Patent Division. They were almost certainly supplied by the law stationers Sackett and Ruscoe, in which Thomas Ruscoe's uncle was a partner. (This was an arrangement among several condemned by the investigators in 1864.) Several of these writers joined the staff; out of 23 in 1859[24], at least eight were former writers. A "folio" of 72 or 90 words cost three-halfpence. Nearly £5,000 was paid for copying in the first two years, probably to the same firm. In 1863, a mere two orders[25] from the Specification Division to the Stationery Office included a thousand quill pens and a dozen boxes of steel pens.

The specifications were printed, like most of the publications, by the Queen's Printers, Eyre and Spottiswoode, conveniently nearby in East Harding Street. Proofs were checked by staff working in pairs, work in which Library staff sometimes assisted. Current specifications were usually on sale within a few weeks.

Technical drawings accompanying specifications were reproduced by lithography. Many of the earliest are subscribed "R. Prosser, Lith". Richard Prosser has been mentioned above as associated with Woodcroft in patent reform proposals. He has been described as contractor for the lithography rather than the artist. This was another instance of an element of improvisation in the early working of the Office; it sought assistance where it was to hand. The arrangement incensed William Day[26], "Lithographer to the Queen" who complained that he had been excluded from tendering and denied work despite lower costs, also that Prosser had failed to do work which he, Day, could have done in London. After this the Office invited tenders in a printed notice. Much of the later lithography was done by the firm of Malby and Son.

Prosser was a popular man of wide interests, and a notable patentee. His contribution to the Patent Office Library, and his son's career in the Office will be described in chapters 7 and 14.

Notes to Chapter 5

1 147 applications   from patents published. Actual applications may of course have been more.

2 sets of rules   Commissioners' Rules, 1852-. BLSRIS SC.

3 By 1854   Collection of notices and circulars. BLSRIS SC. Several reprint earlier dated notices, thus providing a "*terminus post*" but are undated.

4 to prepare three   Patent Law Amendment Act, Schedule.
   documents

5 The Petition was   the charge was printed boldly on the form.
   stamped

6 though halved soon   *Commissioners' Report*, 1852/3, p. 14.

7 being brought by cab   Harding, notebook, recording conversation with former staff member (Neale), in 1925. BLSRIS SC.

8 statement by Edmunds   *Second Report of the Clerk of the Patents*, Hindmarch-Greenwood papers (unsorted) PRO TS 18/536.

9 the Warrant   Collection of original patent documents, BLSRIS SC.

10 A grant for 1865   No 2789, to William Whittle for "new and improved machinery for the manufacture of nails". BLSRIS, SC, Collection of original patent documents.

11 Paid the sealer   *Commissioners' Report*, 1852/3, p. 20.

12 Edmunds recorded   *Second Report of the Clerk of the Patents*, PRO TS 18/536.

13 special payments were *Commissioners' Report*, 1857, p.7.
   made

14 manuscript indexes do Index of Specifications of Patents PRO (C20) 1849-
   not distinguish   1855. Copy, BLSRIS SC.

15 Traditionally payment Gomme, *Patents of Invention*, as cited, pp. 16-18.
   had been made

16 In February, 1853, an Act 16 Vict. c.5.

17 Inland Revenue was   1st Annual Report, 1856 (1857) p. 29.
   gratified

18 Ruscoe described his   *Papers Relating to the Patent Office* (Hindmarch
   visits   Greenwood Report) Minutes, 2.6. 1864, p.82.

19 "blue deed" stamps   Frank, Samuel B., and Schonfield, Josef, *The Stamp Duty of Great Britain and Ireland*, a Catalogue...Vol.I, N.Y. 1970.

20 halved the scale of fees *Commissioners' Report*, 1852/3, p.14.

31

21 Edmunds plausibly claimed   *The History of the Edmunds Scandal*, 1859 p.7.

22 styled themselves "examiners"   *Papers Relating to the Patent Office* (Hindmarch-Greenwood Report) Minutes, 15.6.1864 Q.262, Mr Elwin.

23 in 1855 the small specification staff   *Commissioners' Report*, 1855, p.4.

24 out of 23 in 1859   Patent Office. Annual returns of staff, unpublished.

25 In 1863, a mere two orders   *Statement by the Clerk of the Patents in answer to Woodcroft's letter of the 4th of November, 1863.* PRO, TS 18/536.

26 William Day, Lithographer   *The Times*, March 25, 1855.

6 Patents for everyman? Publishing, libraries and the press

During its first twelve years the Office quadrupled its staff to handle a sixfold increase in applications, while establishing publications that are familiar to the present day patentee. Between 1853 and 1858 Woodcroft organised the transcription and publication of more than 13,000 grants and specifications deep in the public record repositories. The twice-weekly *The Patent Journal* was commenced. The Patent Office Library at Southampton Buildings and the Patent Office Museum at South Kensington were established and the foundation laid for international exchange of patent records. Thanks to the improving spirit of the times – which had brought it into being – there was an unsurpassed level of public interest in the new office and its donated publications, the latter so perfectly in accord with the aspirations behind the new public libraries and influencing their growth. On the other hand, despite these achievements, there was still widespread dissatisfaction with patent law and the system as a whole, and realisation that reform left many problems unsolved. The amendment associations were still active with meetings and petitions. By 1856 the failure to use the mounting surplus revenues[1] for the benefit of the Office, and the large payments to the Law Officers were under fire. There would soon be new enquiries.

Meanwhile this was Woodcroft's age; the early history of the Office is largely an account of his innovations. It sometimes seems as though he is directing the Commissioners, rather than the reverse. He exploited good relations with the press to foster a favourable reception for the Office and its publications, on which his name usually appears. One notice on his retirement made the point: "Mr Woodcroft was a person of strikingly liberal and original views, and inventors owe him much"[2]. It should nevertheless be remembered that he was carrying out the intentions of many other reformers, expressed in the 1852 Act.

Before 1852 Britain was probably worse off than some other European countries in official publication of patent information. One of the few official sources was the abstracts of specifications published in the

Record Office Rolls Chapel reports. Specifications were published at greater length in a few journals. The only indexes, apart from manuscript ones in the Record Office, were private ventures such as Woodcroft's. The French series[3], *Description des Machines et Procédés Specifiés dans les Brévets d'Invention* went back to 1799, though it was printed slightly later. The United States, predictably, had a large Patent Office from 1837, and its annual Commissioner's Report contained classified lists of patents and other information.

Woodcroft had had early aspirations to technical publishing[4]; he now had the official resources to realise them. The Amendment Act required publication of specifications and indexes and their distribution "to such Public Libraries and Museums" as the Commissioners might think fit. In Woodcroft's hands this became the warrant for a remarkable and for its time probably unique programme of Government publishing, in which specifications, indexes and related publications were sold at cost price or freely donated to be made available without charge. The main impulse in donating to libraries, Mechanics Institutes and workplaces (such as railway stations) was certainly, in the spirit of the time, to help the "operative" gain useful knowledge when formal technical education was in short supply. But in distributing this rather specialised information so widely there was a quixotic belief characteristic of the man that some technical knowledge was part of a proper education.

Among the more ambitious clauses in the Amendment Act, clause XXXII is specially demanding, requiring publication of indexes and specifications "heretofore and hereafter". Woodcroft's indexes are not referred to but they are the presence behind this measure, having been shown to the 1851 enquiry and their principles published. Under the supplementary Act of 1853 they were now the property of the nation so there was an obligation to publish them as soon as possible. He had explained how he compiled them by obtaining "from the Lord Chancellor's clerk a list of all the titles of patents ever granted; chronologically arranged they almost fill four folio books"[5].

Clerks in the Chancellor's Patent Office and in others such as the Signet and Privy Seal kept a record of daily business in "docquet books": a docquet was an abstract, either as a separate document or logged in a book. In the case of patents it would be the title or summary. Here is one from the Signet Office book[6].

A lycence for the Erle of Cumberland to transport 100 tonnes of cast yron ordonnance, so as th'one half thereof exceed not the sacre, nor the other half the Mynion... (1591)

Writing at the end of the 19th century, the Librarian, E.W. Hulme[7], stated that Woodcroft's task was assisted by the existence of a manuscript calendar at the old Patent Office in Quality Court, "where a record of grants dating from the year 1617 appears to have been kept with some regularity by the Clerk of Letters Patent down to the year 1851".

Extracts from these MS calendars, supplemented by a collation of certain other manuscript and printed calendars and indexes of specifications kept in the different offices of record combined to form the Chronological Index published in the years 1853-54.

The offices of record were the Rolls Chapel, Enrolment Office and Petty Bag office. Just how Woodcroft did what others apparently had been unable to do is still far from clear. Because the patents and specifications were selected for publication on the basis of his indexes, the first published series runs from 1617 to 1852, misleading many into supposing that the earliest invention patent was granted in 1617.

All the three parts of the index were published between January 1854 and July 1855. The first was the two volume *Titles of Patents of Invention Chronologically Arranged*, long because the titles were often lengthy, followed by the one volume *Alphabetical Index of Patentees with Brief Titles of their Inventions*, the three volume set selling at 30s. Publication of the *Subject Matter Index Made from Titles Only* was delayed until October 1854 because priority was given to a War Department request – see below. The qualification "from titles only" was a warning that the classification was imperfect. The two volumes sold at £2.16.6d, the relatively high price being explained by Woodcroft as the result of a small print run – a dig at Edmunds perhaps. In July 1855 the set was complete with publication of a *Reference Index of Patents*, 1 volume at 30s, the best evidence for Woodcroft's industry. It gives sources of published information on each patent as serially numbered in the *Chronological Index*, from technical journals, law reports, Record Office reports and books. The office of enrolment is included in each case. This concordance to pre-reform patents also pointed out "such of the specifications of patents granted since 14 James I as have been pub-lished by order of the Commissioners" for this project was under way.

Here was a notable early attempt to access a large body of technical information. All the indexes and some other publications were in the Imperial Octavo format; the name is appropriate to publications by the government of the Queen Empress but derives from the folding of an Imperial sheet into eight leaves, somewhat larger than the usual octavo. At first they were sold from the printers, but soon were available at the Office. Woodcroft's name as author appears prominently on all of them and on the subsequent annual indexes, an idiosyncrasy that lasted until his retirement.

In founding *The Patent Journal* Woodcroft improved on the Amendment Act requirement to advertise grants of provisional protection and notices of intention to proceed (clauses XI and XII). The *Journal* commenced publication on January 7, 1854 and was remarkably a twice-weekly appearing on Tuesdays and Thursdays. It contained notices of patents, provisional or granted, items of home and foreign industrial news including patent law, and notices of other Office publications and services. It cost 2d a copy. It was edited by William Green Atkinson, the first Librarian, who had joined the staff the same month. In an account of his duties[8] he included,

> Compiling the Official Journal of the Commissioners, published twice every week, with the attendant examinations and corrections for press. Obtaining foreign and colonial patent laws and Regulations from various official sources: correspondence with subscribers and official contributors.

He is on record[9] as editing the Journal until his death in 1881.

In 1856 the Office was involved in a minor but interesting development in international bibliography. At the time that Woodcroft was developing means of accessing patent information, an official of the Prussian Patent Office in Berlin, Dr E.L. Schubarth, was completing for publication the first volume of his *Repertorium der Technischen Literatur*. This was a classified author-and-title bibliography drawing on a wide range of scientific, technical and patent literature from the resources of the Royal Prussian Ministry for Industry. Commenced in 1824, it covered literature from 1823 to 1856. The Queen's Printers, for the Patent Office, brought out a 25-page preface to the *Repertorium* in which Schubarth's subject headings are translated and related to the corresponding pages in

Woodcroft's recently published Index. The *Repertorium* was published in the United Kingdom by Trubner's, with a preface pointing out that the additional pages enabled official publications of English patents to be consulted where Schubarth's private publications only had abstracts. It rather grandly concluded that the two "leave little doubt that the great desideratum of placing the entire mass of the industrial information of the world within the reach of every mechanic will ultimately be attained".

Considerably later, in 1866, the Office went some way to making foreign literature more accessible by starting its own "current contents" series, *Index to Foreign Scientific Periodicals* contained in the Free Public Library of the Patent Office. "This knowledge", Woodcroft wrote[10], "is diffused through so many channels and hidden under languages so various as to be difficult of access even to the rich and learned, whilst it is entirely beyond the reach of the operative classes". The Index printed as they stood, but with titles translated, the contents lists of the periodicals. It appeared fortnightly, but with half-yearly cumulations, indexed by author and subject. It was compiled by the Office translator, Dr A. Tolhausen. Demand proved less than Woodcroft's advertisement in the first issue suggests, as it closed in 1876.

There are many references in the Commissioners' annual reports to the "great work" of publishing the pre-reform patents which was soon begun with extraordinary determination. It has been widely seen as the outstanding achievement of the Office in the 19th century.

It was facilitated by the fact that the Master of the Rolls was also a Patent Commissioner.

Woodcroft approached the Record Office for facilities immediately on his return from a visit to the northern industrial towns in February 1853 (as described below in connection with the Patent Museum) and soon encountered problems. He wrote to Romilly[11], complaining that the Rolls Chapel staff required written permission from him before the rolls could be copied. The Petty Bag Office and Enrolment Office had been more helpful.

Like the Patent Office, the Public Record Office was a product[12] of long overdue reform. After a series of Record Commission enquiries between

1800 and 1837, the Rolls Estate beside Chancery Lane had been vested in the Crown as the site of a central Record Office for material then dispersed in the Tower and elsewhere. The historian and archivist Sir Francis Palgrave was appointed Deputy Keeper in 1838. The first part of James Pennethorne's attractive Gothic Record Office had been commenced in 1851, and building must have been taking place during Woodcroft's foray among the records.

Romilly gave his permission[13] for the rolls to be copied in ink. (Restrictions evidently applied.) Transcribing the specifications and copying the drawings involved sending writers, proof readers and lithographers into the Rolls Chapel. Later demolished, this repository was the chapel attached to Rolls House, official residence of the Master of the Rolls.

Three groups were involved, one from Woodcroft's staff, one from the lithographers now Malby and Son, and one, listed as Ruscoe's, from the law stationers. All their names were submitted[14] to the Record Office for approval.

The method of working[15] was described by the keeper in the Rolls Chapel[16], H.G. Holden. "One subject or series is taken up at a time..." (perhaps to facilitate the compilation of the abridgments series soon to be published.)

> ...and the Steam Engine or Motive Power is the subject now in hand. Imprimis, Mr Woodcroft's clerks search the calendars from the earliest period to the latest, select references and give directions for the Specifications to be looked out. Mr Woodcroft's clerks inspect the Specifications so looked out and take account of them previously to give directions for copying. The Lithographic Draughtsman inspects the drawings related to the said Specifications and requires them to be unattached from the Rolls for convenience in copying. The Writer inspects the same specifications and takes account of the descriptive matter to be transcribed. The Draughtsman sends his assistants to make copies of the Drawings. The Writer's assistants proceed to copy the descriptions. The Lithographer examines the copies made by his assistants previously to being lithographed. Mr Woodcroft's clerks examine the lithographed proofs with the originals. The readers from HMPO examine the printed proofs of

the descriptive matter in the enrolments. The time of the working men (Gay and Mars) is wholly occupied every day in attending to the above duties. After the subject on hand is concluded the drawings are reattached to the rolls, especial care being required that none are lost or misplaced, the rolls are then rolled up and put away in their proper places. All which occupies so much time that I sometimes find it necessary to suspend the commencement of a new subject until the arrears occasioned by the former has been cleared. The amount of work which I am informed the Commissioners propose doing is of such magnitude and they will require it to be done with so much despatch that the accommodation which the present conveniences of this office can afford will be by no means adequate either as to room or attention.

Woodcroft's approach to the records by subject seems likely to have prolonged the work, entailing repeated retrieval of the same rolls. Records (from the other repositories were also required. In his annual reports Holden made much of the burdens imposed by the Patent Office. His concerns were justified; he had to report[17] to Palgrave that rolls had been damaged with ink, but "no one would confess or impeach". After this, the names of individual copyists had to be submitted for approval. There was a shortage of space, and Palgrave had to ask the Office of Works to cut a doorway[18] into some offices attached to the Chapel. Services were still held there, causing further problems.

The volume of work was greatest[19] in 1855 and 56; in the latter year over three million words were copied, and 1500 drawings (it has been suggested that the lithographic stones used were unprecedently large, but engineering drawings at the time were often very large). Woodcroft witnessed the completion of the last drawing[20] in the Rolls Chapel on the 19th of July, 1858.

As published, the series that resulted, *Letters Patent and Specifications of Letters Patent from March 2nd, 1617 to September 30th, 1852*, contains the text of grant or specification of 14, 399 patents. They are stylishly printed, including scribal abbreviations, the names of patent clerks, and the location of seals.

The approach to the old specifications by single subject made possible the early publication of sets of specifications. The Home Department had requested[21] those concerned with smoke prevention devices and, a mid-century preoccupation, drainage ceramics for sewage. The Admiralty demanded those on ship propulsion. The idea was to publish each set with an introductory historical "appendix". The choice of inventions for mechanical reaping was Woodcroft's own. The subject was topical; the American McCormick machine had been shown at the Exhibition of 1851. This was the only Appendix actually completed. His Foreword is a canonical statement of his belief that the historical study of inventions is the way to improvements; the compilation contained "the accumulated knowledge of mankind in this important department of industry". Set and appendix were sold at £2.3s 11d.

The War Department had requested past and current specifications for firearms, ammunition and related machinery. In 1854 Richard Prosser was giving evidence[22] to the Commons Select Committee on Small Arms. Woodcroft commissioned him to write the Appendix, which was to include an account of the machinery used at the Imperial Russian Arms Factory at Tula. Prosser died suddenly in May 1854, leaving only his notes[23], proofs of the intended drawings, and an unfinished translation of a Russian treatise on the factory. The set, without Appendix, was advertised at £9.18s 6d.

No example of such sets of full specifications for smoke prevention or for marine propulsion survives in the science or humanities collections of the British Library. The material would be published in shorter form in the Abridgments series.

During the nineteenth century the Government sponsored a commendable programme of publication of the public records, through the Record Office and other bodies such as the Historical Manuscripts Commission; publication had gone hand in hand with reform of the care and organisation of the records. In this context Woodcroft's publication of the pre-1852 patents is distinctive as being undertaken to satisfy an urgent practical need rather than historical research.

His *Chronological Index* and published specifications remained authoritative and were not assailed until 1932 when, in a notable paper, A.A. Gomme demonstrated[24] that the Index was defective as a strict guide to the sequence of patents passing the Great Seal.

Not only do mistakes appear to have been made in transcribing the dates of patents from the docquet book entries, but many of the actual MS entries in these books are themselves inaccurately dated – at least in the sense that they do not agree with the dates on the enrolments and on other original documents relating to the granting of the patents – and these inconsistencies and errors have been repeated in the printed records.

Many mistakes in the year of grant arose from the fact that before the introduction of the new calendar in 1752, the legal year ran from March to March and patents dated in the first three months of the year belong in the modern calendar to the following year. Gomme showed that Woodcroft's patent no 1 (Rapburne and Burges patent for engraving maps) was chronologically fifth in the series. Patents in the public records are the end-product of a family of related documents and by using, for instance the Chancery warrant for the Great Seal which was endorsed with the date of receipt by the Chancellor himself he obtained the real date of grant.

Impressive though Gomme's work is, it could be said that, though priority now is of such concern, the priority of long-dead patentees is academic, and Woodcroft at least brought the technical content into the public domain promptly and efficiently.

The first abridgments series

Patent specifications are filed in a single chronological series by country, regardless of subject. During much of the 19th century the Office was concerned with the problem of how to make this information accessible to the searcher, who will be interested in only a fraction of it, but who will want that fraction in some detail.

In 1859 the Office was able to issue a small but striking two-colour poster advertising "ABRIDGMENTS (in classes and chronologically arranged) of all SPECIFICATIONS of patented inventions, from the earliest enrolled to those published under the Act ... to enable the humblest of inventors to examine for himself whether his discovery has been previously patented or not".

41

The series of classified abridgments, the "little red" volumes begun under Woodcroft are still regarded affectionately by the patent professions as the first of the many. (It has been said that he invented abridgments but there was a possible model in the calendars of state papers being published by his acquaintances at the Record Office.) They attempt to cover pre-1852 as well as the "new law" patents in a single volume, possible only before the flood of new patents became too large.

Some details of their publication are now obscured by rebinding; they are "little red abridgments" because of the former Patent Office Library set; they were almost certainly in paper-cover blue book attire originally. Curiously they do not follow the classification used in Woodcroft's index. Each volume has a name-index of patentees and a subject index listing them under each subdivision of the main subject.

The first to appear, appropriately for this sanitation-conscious age, was *Drain Tiles and Pipes* (1857) with a preface by Woodcroft:

> The Indexes to patents are now so numerous and costly as to be placed beyond the reach of a large number of inventors to whom they have become indispensable. To obviate this difficulty, short abstracts or abridgments of the specifications of patents under each head of invention have been prepared separately, and so arranged as to form at once a Chronological, Subject Matter, Reference and Alphabetical Index to the class to which they relate...

Before special staff were appointed in the 1870s, most of the abridgments volumes were written by freelances engaged by Woodcroft. Some were young barristers such as John Macgregor (1825-1892) and John Coryton (1826-1896). Macgregor compiled the first edition of the class *Marine Propulsion*. He became famous as the explorer, canoeing pioneer and philanthropist Rob Roy. Coryton had recently published a work on patent law and went on to become a recorder and judge in India. He compiled the first set of abridgments on *Letterpress Printing* a work which has been reprinted by the Printing Historical Society and has become a collector's item. This class shows the extent and difficulties of the abridgments project. The first volume, Coryton's, was published in 1859 with a preface by Woodcroft; it covers specifications from 1533 to 1857, with an appendix of one missed specification. A further volume appeared in 1878 with a preface by Reader Lack (by then Woodcroft's successor) and covering specifications 1858–1866. This has two appendices or supplements, the first covering 1810–1857, the second of just one patent. Another volume was published under Lack in 1880, covering 1867–1876. (Both the later volumes were titled Part 2.) An unquantifiable part of these was the work of a Mr Rae.

Among other abridgers, Dugald Campbell, who compiled *Preservation of Food, Bleaching and Dyeing, Paper Manufacture*, taught chemistry at University College London, and R.S. Meikleham was the occasional writer "Robert Stuart". Nathanael Barnabe who did the *Shipbuilding* volume, later became Admiralty Head of Naval Construction. Theodore Aston (d.1910) compiled the *Fire Arms* volume.

Some of the abridgments volumes include details of patents predating Woodcroft's official series, drawing from such sources as the Record Office calendars, and Rymer's *Foedera*. A few, such as *Printing*, have historical introductions, gallant attempts at instant scholarship, full of miscellaneous information from antiquity onwards. Aston included a puff for Patent Office publications. Woodcroft wrote the introduction to Class 1, *Drainage* and is still worth reading on the London sewers. The industrious Marwick Michell, Woodcroft's senior clerk, was the general editor and also a compiler.

In early 1858 Woodcroft wrote to the Chancellor,[25] Lord Cranworth, more than once for a ruling on payment for abridgers, pointing out that some of the work was being done "by the Commissioners' servants". They agreed on a fee of 7s per specification. The authors were not credited on the titles, Woodcroft's was the only name, but they earned substantial amounts: MacGregor was paid £281 for *Marine Propulsion*, selling at 4s, and ruefully noted in his journal[26] that his name did not appear. The amounts paid[27] certainly concerned one Chancellor, Lord Westbury, who told an enquiry[28] that he "put a stop to them" and evidently had little idea of their value to patentees. They continued to be written partly by non-staff until the 1870s, when pressure for improved search-aids resulted in the appointment of special staff.

For a time in the 1860s and until more staff were available, applicants were required to supply their own abridgments[29], for publication in quarterly and annual cumulations. The prefaces to these volumes confessed that the entries were printed as they stood, "no attempt being made to correct errors in spelling or grammatical construction". Inevitably, some supplied "abridgments" amounting to complete specifications. It had been a policy of desperation.

During the first two decades, complaints at the shortcomings of indexes and abridgments were prominent in the many petitions[30] sent to the Commissioners or the government. It was felt that they should be the responsibility of the Office, and not the patentee. This problem of satisfactory search aids was not solved during the Commissioners' existence, and a start was not made until the appointment of technically qualified staff in 1878. Even then there were problems with the system.

Reprints of scarce pamphlets

A publishing project that had a short life but exemplified the early zeal of the Office, was the printing of additions to the published patents "consisting for the most part of reprints of scarce pamphlets descriptive of early patented inventions". These prospectuses of inventors of earlier centuries were published in the stylish blue book format of the specifications, sold either singly for a few pence or as a set at 9s 6d, with a lavish title page and Woodcroft's name under the royal arms. As it happened, only one set was published, curiously made up, continuously paged but with individual covers. It included Simon Sturtevant's *Metallica* (1612) and the Marquis of Worcester's *Exact and True Definition of the Stupendous Water-Commanding Engine* (c.1661). A few were from the Library's originals, others are reprints of reprints.

Early in this century, Henry Trueman Wood, Secretary of the Society of Arts, remembered translating[31] one item from the Latin for Woodcroft, *The Letter of Master William Drummond for the Construction of Machines, Weapons and Engines of War* ... (1626), in fact part of a Scottish patent of Charles I, containing sixteen unspecified inventions. Wood, a clerk in the Office at the time, was not credited with the translation.

This one-off collection of tracts is another pleasing example of official printing, reproducing all the drawings, and giving a glimpse into the projector's world just before the industrial revolution had gathered momentum.

Patents for everyman – the donation programme

The Office had been mandated in the Amendment Act to donate its publications "to such public libraries and Museums as they (the Commissioners) shall think fit". By 1855 we find that[32]:

> The Commissioners have transmitted the prints of specifications, indexes of patents and all other papers printed by them to the chief magistrates and corporations of the principal towns within the United Kingdom, to be placed in such public libraries as may now exist or may hereafter be formed for the purpose...

stipulating on a printed form of acceptance, that the publications be in the charge of a responsible librarian, be available free of charge "on any pretext whatsoever" and never loaned or removed. The Commissioners claimed that the gift "has in most cases laid the foundations of public free libraries where none previously existed".

As well as being closely contemporary, there were affinities between the movements for public libraries and patent reform. One common aim was the improvement of manufacturing.

Between 1835 and the passing of the Public Libraries Act[33] in 1850 there were several attempts to legislate for rate-funded public institutions, among their aims being to "embrace the means of diffusing literature and scientific information". William Ewart, the father of the Public Libraries Act and its prototype the 1845 Museums Act, had chaired a Select Committee on Arts and Manufactures in 1835-6 which made similar recommendations. The first decade of the Patent Office was also that of the first major civic libraries such as Manchester's and Liverpool's[34] in 1852, as well as many others improvised on existing institutions. It was logical that officially published "useful knowledge" should join the stock of the new libraries; such a proposal had been made many years earlier by the author of *A Manual for Mechanics Institutions*[35], published by the Society for the Diffusion of Useful Knowledge.

At its inception the donation programme had a public impact unique in the history of the Office. Society, especially the new urban and civic society in the mid-century was unprecedently conscious of invention and of the value of the new libraries and museums in raising the lot and the morals of the people. There was something about the nature and liberal scale of the gesture of donation that chimed with the mood of the time. (Euphoria at mechanism sometimes went over the top: the Science and Art columnist of *The Birmingham Journal*[36] combined a review of Owen Jones' famous *Grammar of Ornament* with proposals for a National Portrait Gallery and notice of Patent Office donations. "The examples are so rich and missal like" he wrote of the chromolithography, that "a mediaeval illuminator would drown himself in despair") Specifications of historic as well as new inventions served a dual Victorian interest. Interest in the Office was also stimulated by the unfamiliar phenomenon of annual reports from a government office and by press reviews of individual publications: Woodcroft's *Appendix to Reaping Machines* gave rise to a number of articles on invention and agriculture in the provincial press, the City newspaper *The Mark Lane Express*[37], and *The Athenaeum*. In a *Quarterly Review* article on the Commissioners' publications, Thomas Webster[38] lauded "a copious stream, drawn off in a multitude of channels, penetrating the country in all directions." and irrigating it with fertilising information".

Commendation of the beneficial effect of the Commissioners' policy came from some unlikely quarters. *The Philanthropist*[39], in a leader on crime and the social value of "popular and useful instruction" cited the Great Exhibition, adding, "we think the liberal provisions of the Patent Law Amendment Act hold forth great encouragement".

This was the period of Woodcroft's greatest prominence as a civil servant and shows the extent to which the Commissioners' policy was really his own. The conditions laid down for donations were a useful lever to move dilatory local government in the direction of free libraries. He used his contacts with local people and the press to good effect. His technique was to feed local journals with press reports or correspondence from successful donations elsewhere. In 1856 *The Glasgow Examiner* castigated[40] the city Corporation for withholding publications sent several months earlier, and reprinted, in addition to their correspondence with Woodcroft, reports from libraries in Manchester, Newcastle, Kidderminster and the Marylebone Free Library in London.

The provincial impact of Patent Office publications, and the Southampton Buildings-provincial city axis is best exemplified by the situation in Manchester and Salford, where of course Woodcroft was well known. The earliest recipient of the three sets of specifications and drawings already published was his acquaintance the consulting engineer Benjamin Fothergill who displayed them at his office[41]. Soon there was pressure to take advantage of the Commissioners' offer and the civic authorities in Manchester and Salford drafted petitions in favour[42] of donations to the Chetham's and new Royal Free Library, and for Salford to the Peel Park Library and City Mechanics Institution.

Woodcroft forestalled them[43], writing on February 23rd, 1855, that "the Commissioners of Patents had granted all their works to the Chetham Free Library and Royal Free Library of Manchester". He enclosed copies of his exchanges with the Commissioners represented by Sir John Romilly. The latter had conferred with the Chancellor and agreed that Woodcroft's indexes could be given to the principal manufacturing towns but asked for a list. Woodcroft responded ironically, "as your honour has only mentioned indexes I fear I have made some mistake as to what 'the public so much desire and stand in need of'", citing the Amendment Act's reference to "all specifications". "What the public so much require is the whole of the Commissioners' publications". What Romilly thought of this exchange being published in *The Manchester Guardian* is not on record. He replied curtly, permitting donations to Manchester and Salford, adding that he would consult the Chancellor concerning the others.

Woodcroft's letter to the Mayor[44] conveys the scale of the gift: "Sir, three series of the Commissioners' publications are arranged ready to be delivered here to any agent who may be appointed in town. If one agent could act for the three libraries it would save considerable time, labour and confusion. Each series contains nine volumes of indexes, two volumes of journal, one volume appendix to reaping machines, one volume index to fire arms and 5,600 specifications of patents... three cases will be required about three feet square each.

The Council's vote of thanks to the Commissioners was linked with a hint that more would be welcome, in view of their importance to the working population, and with fulsome expressions of gratitude to Woodcroft, "this former citizen".

During May and June 1855 what was probably the first exhibition[45] of published patents was held in the Free Library. In Sheffield the donation[46] was arranged by the local MP, George Hadfield, who approached the Commissioners via Woodcroft, "whose family are so well known in Sheffield". In Rotherham the Independent Board of Health resolved to accept 200 volumes "to establish a free library", which validates Woodcroft's claim (in the Office reports) that the donations resulted in the creation of new libraries.

Woodcroft made sure that this policy and its reception was as well publicised officially as in the press. In 1856 *The Patent Journal* listed some 80 recipient towns and institutions such as dockyards and ordnance factories and such long lists helped to pad out the Office report, year after year. Curators were asked to state whether the institution was an existing free library, or had modified its rules to comply, its opening hours, readership, and the material most in demand. This latter reflected regional manufactures, as in Kidderminster "where the good people mainly directed their studies to the class of inventions which applied to machinery and looms for carpets". The librarian of the Newcastle "Lit. and Phil." reported that manufacturers and managers sometimes followed the specifications to the binder's shop.

International exchange began with a donation from the US Patent Office early in 1855. Woodcroft notified the US ambassador that the Commissioners would reciprocate with "the works on British patents now published and hereafter to be printed". In this early example of the special relationship, the Office's own red morocco-bound set was delivered in April 1856 to the approval of the Washington press[47]. By 1856 the Office was supplying[48] complete sets of publications to the Colonial Secretary's office for the British colonies and dependencies.

Exchange of information[49] with a number of European patent offices was initiated by Woodcroft during a tour he undertook in the Long Vacation of 1856 and reported to the then Chancellor, Cranworth:

> ...I visited some of the Patent Offices on the Continent to make myself acquainted with the gentlemen who presided over them, and learn their mode of conducting patent business. My object was also to endeavour to bring about a weekly communication between their several departments and this office, in which I was successful in all cases".

48

He stressed that these officers were in favour of harmonisation of law and practice internationally, with proposals to be drawn up at a conference – a notable anticipation of developments later in the century, recalled when his letter to the Chancellor was reprinted in the *Society of Arts Journal* at the time of the Vienna Patent Congress in 1873.

In July 1859, Edmunds' complaints of his extravagance[50] provoked Woodcroft to a defence of his foreign communications,

> From this office there is a correspondence with every government in Europe except Italy, and the United States, with all the British colonies and with all the free libraries to which the Commissioners' works have gone, with patentees in all parts of the British Dominions and I may say all over the world and this is now so well indexed and arranged that any letter received or copy sent out can be had in a moment.

– a pardonable instance of him in bombastic mode. He added, with more restraint than he would show later, "I do not complain of the tone and manner of Mr Edmunds in his intercourse with me, but it is certainly not so courteous as that of the Commissioners".

Woodcroft had an unusual interest in the geography of invention. In 1859 the Office printed an elaborate volume *Showing the Number of Patents of Invention Granted in England and Wales from AD 1617 to AD 1852* (Sept. 30) – the AD is a nice touch – an analysis of the locations of inventors consisting of large folded sheets showing the names of every town and village in the world that had produced a grantee of a British patent and in vertical columns the number of patents in any given year between 1617 and 1852. One set of tables showed them in numerical order with London heading the list with 13,678 patents and another by place. A second set of tables continued the lists for the new law patents up to 1858. This work was not advertised among the Commissioners' publications and the former Patent Office Library copies are the only ones in the British Library. Harding called the work a tribute to Woodcroft's enthusiasm but added "it may have been somewhat misdirected". There is a similar MS volume for the UK only.

It may have helped in deciding the distribution of publications. In 1878 the Office reported[51] donations of complete sets to more than 130

institutions at home and abroad and another 300+ of abridgments. Consignments were made up for collection by agents for the libraries in the warehouse or "iron house" behind the Office. In 1864, Edmunds recorded[52], Samuel Casserley, a writer, was "attending the agents of the public libraries and writing the tablets for each parcel.
Prints are distributed to the several libraries once in the week".

The implied scale of the operation for a small institution is extraordinary, especially as regards the current specifications. This Great Eastern of a project was over ambitious, however well meant, and by the 1870s was being recognised as such. The ever hardheaded *Engineering*[53] complained at such lavishness at the ultimate expense of the British patentee.

> We find for example that no less than eleven sets, each of which costs upward of £3,000 ... go to the United States.

> We sincerely trust that these lavish gifts are appreciated, and that the 'Dorsetshire labourer! for instance is in the habit of frequently refreshing what mind he has by a perusal of the blue books at his county town. It is quite to be expected that the fashionables of Leamington, wearied with fetes and archery meetings in the Jephson Gardens, turn with delight to the specifications in their town hall.

Such philistinism was not general. In 1877 the Office itself[54] was pulping surplus specifications. Woodcroft privately protested.

Binding of valued material[55] was a problem for some libraries. In 1889 there were urgent exchanges between the Newcastle Library Committee and the Librarian concerning costs. To prevent delay, the Patent Office was issuing specifications unbound. It was felt that donated official publications should not be a charge on the Library. In this instance, the Corporation paid. The perennial issue of Patent Office surplus revenue was sometimes raised in this connection. In the modern period there has certainly been some disposal of patent publications by libraries, just how much it would be interesting to know. The modern equivalent of these donations, the Patent Information Network, is on a more modest scale.

Printing costs inevitably formed a very large part of overall Patent Office costs. In 1854 the head of the Stationery Office[56], J.R. McCulloch, told an enquiry into Government printing that work for the Office had cost

£56,000[57] a year much of it for lithography. Similar figures appear in the Commissioners' reports. Woodcroft and Edmunds, at this time in harmony, agreed to use a cheaper paper and to consolidate the type. "So far as I can judge", McCulloch reported, "they have shown every desire to diminish the cost". (In the same year, *Hansard* had been paid £24,590.)

A favourable press

The opening of a new public office in London, with a free library – it formally opened in March 1855 – the new publications and annual reports resulted in an unrepeated level of interest and favourable comment. Both its ambience and working were portrayed by reporters sent to Southampton Buildings. Interest was not limited to the specialist press, it extended to dailies like *The Times* and *Morning Post*, and even the political reviews, *The Quarterly* and *Westminster Review* linked to the still current question of whether patents were for or against the public good.

The best known account[58] and the source of my title is *A Room Near Chancery Lane*, in Dickens' journal *Household Words* in 1857. Better known for fiction, the journal also published on current affairs in industry and business. The author, George Dodd[59], specialised in factual and documentary pieces and contributed more than fifty to *Household Words*, only part of his output before (like many a "miscellaneous writer") being found dead in his rooms in drab Torriano Avenue, Kentish Town. Dodd's tone, typical of the time, was that things administrative and legal were out of joint, but with redeeming aspects.

> There is a formidable number of rooms near Chancery Lane, where vexation of spirit attends the steps of those who find themselves involved in proceedings in law and (so called) equity, but one particular room is now in our thoughts – small and neat, indicative of improvement – in one among many things woefully in need of being improved.

He describes the origin, working and output of the Office: the Patent Journal is "a patentees newspaper" and the publications "form the nucleus of what may one day be the most valuable industrial library in the kingdom". The "indefatigable Mr Woodcroft" is publishing all the specifications. After a favourable account of the Library – the room of his title – he concludes cautiously,

> Let the controversy for and against patents take what turn it may, this room near Chancery Lane marks one improvement…it does not sever us from contact with routine and red tape, but it renders those unpopular symbols less obstructive and annoying than before.

A *Morning Post*[60] leader the same year was devoted to the Commissioners' report and stressed the increase in patenting since the reform. "The Office", it commenced, "was destined to accomplish results of the highest benefit to the nations".

Many early accounts of the Office (like many since) took the chance to satirise the Chaffwax era, and to describe the diversity of past inventions revealed by publication. *The Times*[61] in late 1858 differed only in the superior quality of the writing:

> In a dingy part of Chancery Lane is a little court, duller and more dingy even than the parent thoroughfare. It is a solitary byway apparently leading nowhere in particular, where even ragged children shun playing as though it was something too sombre even for their capabilities of rousing into noise. Gaunt, smoke blackened houses are on either side, the cheerless doors of which are rendered still more formidable by names of legal firms in sharp white letters like so many rows of teeth, warning the pedestrian not to enter rashly there … At the end of this passage is a low building with two doorways. One is the Great Seal Patent Office; the other, oddly enough, the Office of the Registrar in Lunacy.

A visitor from Printing House Square would use the Quality Court entrance. Unfortunately this one's name is not listed in the archive. Dickensian colour was obligatory when describing Chancery, London at the time. Entering the Library he finds "a smaller and still meaner passage, though one in which, in spite of the masses of books, the most perfect order reigns". Here is an office with a yearly surplus "equal to that of some Principalities".

In describing some of the bizarre and eccentric inventions revealed by the specifications he strikes a satiric note perennially provoked by invention: "the most wonderful records of human ingenuity and sometimes we must add of human folly" – it goes back at least to Swift. One miscellaneous writer, John Timbs[62], adopted the piece for his *Romance of London*. But Woodcroft's indexes here constitute "an ABC to the lives of Watt and Wedgwood, of Crompton and Hargreaves, of Kay and Arkwright, of Cort and Wheatstone". The writer concluded with a hint at a second article, and a plea for a worthy building.

Evidently the public reception of the new Office was generally favourable and sometimes glowing. Professional users were less enthusiastic. Abridgments and indexes were increasingly criticised as part of the growing dissatisfaction with patent administration in the 1860s.

Notes to Chapter 6

1 mounting surplus revenus — Joseph Paxton, in SA *Journal*, Feb, 1856, reprinted, *The Mechanics Magazine*, 9.2.1856.

2 Mr Woodcroft was a person — *Engineering*, 21, 7.4.1876, p.283.

3 the French Series — Rimmer, B., *Official Guide to International Industrial Property Publications*. Ed. S. Van Dulken. BL SRIS 1992.

4 early aspirations to technical publishing — *The Engineer*, 47, 14.2.1879, p 118, "he was to have been a contributor to a periodical called *The Workshop* (obit., by Prosser).

5 from the Lord Chancellor's clerk — Lords Select Committee on the Patent Bills, 1851, Minutes, Q.1564.

6 Signet Office Book — *Transcripts of Entries in the Signet Docket Book*, 1584–1617, Relating to Patents of Invention. BLSRIS SC (46932).

7 the Librarian, E. W. Hulme — *English Patent Law, its History, Literature, and Library*, Library Bureau, London, 1898, p 56. (Reprint, from *The Library*, Feb.–April, 1898).

8 an account of his duties — MS. 1864, Woodcroft Collection, BLSRIS SC.

9 he is on record — Boase, *Modern English Biography*, vol. I.

10 "this knowledge Woodcroft wrote — Advertisement, Vol.I, no.1.

11 He wrote to Romilly — Letter, 26.2.1853, PRO, PRO-1-17.

12 the Record Office was a product. Edwards, Lewis, *A Remarkable Family, the Palgraves*, In Shaftesley, J.M. ed. *Remember the Days, Essays in Anglo-Jewish History*, Presented to J.M.Roth, 1966. Also Commission on the Public Records, General Report, 1837.

13 Romilly gave his permission Letter, 3.3.1853, PRO 1-19.

14 all their names were submitted Lists, Patent Office, Malby and Ruscoe personnel. PRO 1-19.

15 the method of working Holden (of the Rolls Chapel) to Sir F. Palgrave, 8.10.1855, PRO 1-19.

16 the Rolls Chapel background in Maxwell-Lyte, F.C., *Historical Notes on the Great Seal*, HMSO 1926 pp 403-4.

17 he had to report Memo, Holden to Palgrave, PRO 1-19.

18 to cut a doorway Memo, Palgrave to Thornborrow, Board of Works 11.10.1855. PRO 1-19.

19 volume of work was greatest Deputy Keeper of the Public Records, Annual Report, 1856, p.6.

20 the last drawing Woodcroft, *Minute Book*, 19.7.1858. Harding's excerpt. BLSRIS SC.

21 the Home Department had requested Commissioners' Report, 1852/3, p.5.

22 Prosser was giving evidence Select Committee on Small Arms, Report, 1854, Minutes, 21 3 1854, pp 172-184.

23 leaving only his notes *Collection of Memoranda, Letters and Drawings Relating to Fire Arms*…BLSRIS SC (15217).

24 A.A. Gomme demonstrated *Date Corrections of English Patents*, NST XIII, 1932-3, pp 159-164.

25 Woodcroft wrote to the Chancellor Letter, 9.6.1858. Science Museum, Z. 4 Letter Book B, fol.264.

26 noted in his journal Hodder, Edwin, *John Macgregor*, London 1894.

27 payments for abridgments Commissioners' Reports, Incidental Expenses, 1852/3-

28 Lord Westbury who told an enquiry House of Lords, Select Committee (Edmunds Enquiry) Report. 1865. Westbury to Woodcroft, 4.8.1864.

29 to supply their own abridgments Commissioners' Rule, 17.12.1866.

30 the many petitions Collection of petitions (copies), BLSRIS SC.

31 Wood…remembered translating — Letter, H. T. Wood to R.B. Prosser, 21 2.1916. Insert in pamphlet set, BLSRIS SC (2993).

32 By 1855 we find that — Commissioners' Report, 1854, p.6.

33 the Public Libraries Act — Kelly, Thomas, *History of Public Libraries in Great Britain*, L. Association, 1973. pp 14,15.

34 Manchester's and Liverpool's — Kelly, as cited, pp 23-56.

35 *A Manual for Mechanics' Institutions* — Duppa, B.F. (cited Kelly, pp 56, 57.)

36 *The Birmingham Journal* — 5.3.1856.

37 *The Mark Lane Express* — 22.1.1855; 5.3.1855; 1913.1855, 18.6.1855; 20.8.1855. *The Athenaeum*, 7.1.1854..

38 Thomas Webster — *Quarterly Review*, 105, Jan. 1859, p.136-Anonymous.(author from *The Wellesley Index to Victorian Periodicals*.)

39 raising the lot and moral — *The Philanthropist* 2.7.1855.

40 *The Glasgow Examiner* castigated — 23.8.1856.

41 displayed them at his Office — *The Manchester Guardian*, 13.1.1855,

42 petitions in favour — *The Manchester Guardian*, 7.2.1855.

43 Woodcroft forestalled them — Ibid, 7.3.1855.

44 Woodcroft's letter to the mayor — Ibid.

45 the first exhibition — *The Manchester Examiner and Times*, 19, 26 5.1855.

46 in Sheffield the donatino — *Sheffield Independent*, 7.4.1855.

47 International exchange began — *Daily National Intelligencer* (Washington) 26.4.1856.

48 By 1856 the Office was supplying — Supplementary Report, *Patent Journal* 8.8.1856, p.809.

49 Exchange of Information — Royal Commission on the Patent Law, Report, 1864. Appendix 14, p.149.

50 Complaints of his   Woodcroft to Fitzroy Kelly, 27.7.1859, (copy in
    extravagance   Woodcroft to Master of the Rolls, 4.11.1863. PRO TS
                               18-536).

51 In 1878 the Office   Commissioners' Report, Appendix F.
    reported

52 In 1864, Edmunds   *Second Report of the Clerk of the Patents*. PRO TS18-536.
    recorded

53 the ever hardheaded   18, 11.9.1874.
    Engineering.

54 in 1877 the Office itself   Woodcroft to R.B. Prosser, 3.2.1877. In Memorial Book,
                               BLSRIS SC.

55 Binding of valued   Greenwood, Thomas, *Public Libraries*, Cassell, 1891, pp
    material   44,45.

56 the head of the   John Ramsay McCulloch (1789-1864) writer on
    Stationery Office   political economy, said to be the original of
                               Mr Gradgrind, in Dickens' *Hard Times*.

57 had cost £56,000   Enquiry into Government Printing, 1854, Minutes,
                               McCulloch's evidence Q.298.

58 The best known   *Household Words*, 15, 21.2.1857, p.190.
    account

59 George Dodd   George Dodd (1808-1881) miscellaneous writer.
                               Modern English Biography.

60 *The Morning Post*   2.3.1857, p-4.

61 *The Times*   29.12.1858.

62 John Timbs   *Romance of London*, Warne, 1928, Vol. 2.

7 Some largely unrecognised subordinates

By the end of the first ten years, Patent Office staff had increased from the original seven salaried clerks and a few "writers" to some 29, including Woodcroft and Edmunds. (This total includes non-clerical staff such as messengers and warehousemen, all in the Specification Division.) The biggest single increase was in 1859, when ten joined the staff. Several of these however had been on the stationers' payroll. The Specification Division grew to 19, reflecting the importance of the technical, publishing and Library side. The last had opened officially in March, 1855 and rapidly became a much-loved institution, notwithstanding its wretched accommodation.(See Ch.14.)

With applications running at some 3,000 a year, most of the stresses (and the resulting evidence) were on the specification side where the work was the more exacting, comprising the passing of technical texts for press, arranging lithography, the reading-room (such as it was) sales, indexing and donations to the libraries and other institutions. The routine work of the Patent Division seems to have gone smoothly, as Edmunds liked vehemently to claim, calling his division "the Patent Office proper"[1]- an allusion perhaps to the traditional non-invention work. Much of the credit must go to Thomas Ruscoe whom the Lord Chancellor Westbury referred to as a "man of business"[2]. Office hours were normally ten to four with a half day on Saturday – undoubtedly a reason for the desirability of public service jobs. Edmunds stated that he sometimes asked his staff to work a whole Saturday, with "time-in-lieu".

When commenting on Woodcroft's successor Lack in 1876 and pointing out some of the former's virtues and shortcomings, the journal *Engineering*[3] referred to the burden carried of late by "hardworking but unknown and to a great extent unrecognised subordinates".

One of these was certainly William Greene Atkinson (1810-1881)[4], the first Librarian. Born in Darlington, he qualified as a barrister (Middle Temple). He joined the Patent Office as an extra clerk in January 1854. The following year he was promoted as a "skilled mechanical draughtsman" perhaps on the strength of his additional work on specifications. In addition to Library duties — acquisitions, cataloguing, translating titles of foreign journals — he supplied "needful information for readers and others respecting the business of the Office and the working of the Act". He also edited abridgments, negotiated with outside abridgers and edited specifications. Some of the pressure leaks into his own description[5]:

> Preparation of all copies of Specifications, Disclaimers and Articles of Alteration for Her Majesty's printers. Examining each document with a view to fixing an intelligible heading and finally examining and correcting for the press. The matter now dealt with amounts when printed to about 65 Blue Books (i.e. individual specifications) or two thick volumes weekly. This service previous to the opening of the Library and for two years subsequently was performed by Mr Atkinson alone...

Atkinson could have added that he edited *The Patent Journal*, a twice-weekly publication. He had a special interest in the history of printing, which probably accounts for the wealth of such material in the former Patent Office collections. He was probably responsible for the Library acquiring a substantial part of the collection of Jacob Koning, a Dutch historian of printing. E.W. Hulme, Librarian from 1894 to 1920 has recorded that the history of the invention of printing was a hobby of "the first Librarian".

Herbert John Allison (1829-1894) the 2nd Assistant Librarian had been a legal copying clerk; he was appointed an Extra Clerk[6] in the Specification Division (at £78 a year) in 1858, having been in the Office but on the stationer's payroll since 1853. He rose to Junior Clerk at £100 p.a. in 1859. His own description of his work in the Library in modern terms was reader services, shelf maintenance and copying data for official returns. According to one source he also owned[7] a tobacconist's business in Kentish Town from 1864 to 1868, twice becoming bankrupt. Allison succeeded Atkinson when the latter died in 1881, becoming the second Patent Office Librarian until his death. He lived long enough to be involved in the early planning of the new Library in the 1890s. According to tradition he disliked the new examining staff sufficiently to bar them from the Library.

Richard Prosser senior's acquaintance with Woodcroft and his work for the Office has been mentioned above. Following his untimely death in 1854 Woodcroft wrote to his son[8], Richard Bissell Prosser (1838-1918).

Great Seal Patent Office
3rd Octr. 1856

Dear Richard,

I have been a few weeks on the Continent without leaving any word where to write to me, consequently your letters have rested here. Next Monday if you like to come here to make a trial of the duties of this place I will gladly point them out to you. Perhaps it will be most satisfactory for you to make a week's trial without giving it out to any person of your family that it is your intention to leave Birmingham. I should be happy to have offered you a bed but my cottage is now full. Be pleased to make my best respects to all your family.

Strictly, this invitation contravened Her Majesty's Order in Council[9] (1855) following the famous Northcote-Trevelyan Report; it required that "all such young men as may be proposed to be appointed in any junior situation" should take an examination. The same must have applied to several others of the staff; it was still early days for the Civil Service.

Prosser was appointed "extra clerk" at £78 p.a. a few days later. Beginning his career in the Library, he described his duties as "To take charge of the Periodical Works", also to "give attendance in the Reading Room and assist in the general business of the Library". Prosser's later and not always happy career as head of special indexing and of the examining staff is touched on below. His great interest was technical and industrial history. The article series on *Birmingham Inventors and Inventions* reprinted in book form (1881) was only one of many contributions such as pamphlets and DNB entries. As Woodcroft's Boswell, and donor of books and manuscripts to the Library, he has a special place in the history of the Office. His surviving papers on inventors were acquired for the British Museum (now British Library) manuscripts collection.

I have touched in passing on the career of William Marwick Michell (died 1885) below. As Woodcroft's personal assistant almost from the beginning he if anyone was a largely unrecognised subordinate. Before joining he had been assistant editor of *Newton's London Journal* [10], useful experience for his work as editor and compiler of abridgments and of Patent Museum catalogues. His formal title from 1859 was Senior Clerk in the Specification Division.

Another little known but noteworthy member of staff was the Office translator Dr Alexander Tolhausen[11] (c.1819–1887). An example of European career mobility, he was born in Germany; he first practised as a patent agent in London but was briefly appointed translator and interpreter to the French Imperial Court before being invited to work for the Office by Woodcroft. From 1857 to 1866 he was paid "according to the amount of work actually performed"[12]. In July 1866 he joined the staff at a salary of £500 p.a. His varied duties included correspondence, translating foreign patent law for *The Patent Journal*, and – while it lasted – translating titles and subject headings for the *Index to Foreign Scientific Periodicals*. Tolhausen compiled or helped in the compilation of several multilingual technical dictionaries. His Paris-based relative, François Tolhausen acted as an unofficial French agent of the Office, supplying press cuttings.

There is no record of his retirement but one obituary mentioned[13] a report that "his mind was acutely affected by his pension being reduced to one-third of what his long service entitled him to, and from that time he lost his reason". He was another undeserving victim of Treasury stringency and 19th century laissez faire.

Notes to Chapter 7

1 "the Patent Office proper"*A History of the Edmunds Scandal*, 1869, p. 4.

2 Ruscoe... "a man of business"	Lord Westbury to Master of the Rolls, undated. Published in Lords Select Committee on Edmunds resignation, Report, 1865, Minutes, Master of the Rolls evidence.
3 the journal *Engineering* referred	21, 7.4.1876, p. 283.
4 W.G. Atkinson	*Modern English Biography*.
5 his own description	MS, 1864. Woodcroft Collection, BLSRIS SC.

6 Allison...was appointed   Patent Office, Staff Registers, vol.1.
   extra clerk

7 he also owned   *Modern English Biography.*

8 Woodcroft wrote to his   Letter, 3.10.1856. Memorial Book, BLSRIS SC.
   son

9 Order in Council   of 21.5.1855 Regulating the Admission of Persons to the Civil Service. (Text in Reader, K.M. *The Civil Service Commission* HMSO, 1981, Appendix 3.)

10 *Newton's London Journal*   Michell's obituary, *The Engineer*, 59, 27.3.1885, p.288.

11 Tolhausen   Obit., *Iron*, 16.9.1887.

12 according to the   Patent Office, Staff Registers, vol.1.
   amount of work
   actually performed

13 one obituary mentioned   *Iron*, as cited.

8 The Edmunds affair

The situation in which one old-school officer was nominally senior to another who was pushing, innovative and indispensable seemed likely to lead to trouble and so it did. In July, 1859, Edmunds began to interfere in the running of the Specification Division. Perhaps worried about costs, or merely wanting to assert his authority, he laid off eight clerks[1] – presumably the stationers' writers on whom the Office was heavily relying – on the grounds that it was overmanned. He also accused Woodcroft's department of falsifying accounts.

On the 1st of August that year Woodcroft sent a heated justification[2] of his department to Fitzroy Kelly. (Kelly had just ceased to be Attorney General and a patent Commissioner; Woodcroft had evidently forgotten this.) He stressed the large correspondence of his section and threatened to use his influence and demand an enquiry. "I shall move my friends... Mr Edmunds deportment towards me and other officers..renders it quite impossible for any of us to reason with him". He quoted statements from his staff in support.

(I would find the date of this letter dubious, being contrary to other accounts, but it is to Kelly, who had long ceased to be a patent Commissioner in 1863, the usually quoted date for the complaint.)

In April 1861, John Samuel Smith, a clerk engaged in the sale of specifications[3], "was suspended by Mr Woodcroft on suspicion of appropriating to his own use money received in the sale room of printed specifications". According to one account, there had been an anonymous tip-off[4] from outside. Smith, when charged by Edmunds, admitted the fact, and "offered to make out a list of his defalcations"[5]. He was found to have stolen £749.7s, 4d, and was dismissed. The matter had not yet become public (if the Chancellor knew he did nothing) and that May the Office carried out a complicated damage-control operation in which Woodcroft and Duffield (the clerk in charge of Smith) put up the money between them, handed it to Smith in return for a mortgage on some property in Richmond in which he had an interest, so that Smith could pay it back to Woodcroft who paid it in to Edmunds. They also made Smith take out life insurance. The legal side was handled by Woodcroft's solicitors whose costs were also charged to Smith. The whole operation displays a Victorian love of niggling detail and legal formality. (There is evidence that Smith soon began to pay off the mortgage.)

The tenacity with which Smith was pursued is evident from the report of the Treasury Solicitor [6]:

> Cunliffe's nephew (Cunliffe was Woodcroft's solicitor) Duffield and Smith repaired to Richmond, viewed the property, called upon the agent there and inspected the Will under which Smith had correctly claimed his interest. Memoranda were taken of the rents – which turned out to be a little more than Smith had stated (viz. £100 a year). But his interest was already mortgaged for £250 at ten per cent. Messrs Cunliffe prepared a mortgage, a Policy was also effected on Smith's life for £800, premium £21.16s.

In November the following year, 1862, the Chancellor, Lord Westbury (around whose neck the Office was to prove such an albatross) did act. He ordered an investigation by a QC borrowed from the Treasury, John Greenwood. Between the 11th of November and the 1st of December Greenwood interviewed the principal members of staff, making rapid and consequently almost illegible notes in longhand, fair copying them later. (Shorthand was a rare accomplishment, one recalls Charles Dickens' toil learning it for Parliamentary reporting.) He submitted his report in January 1863. It is surprising, in view of the above, to learn that Woodcroft, interviewed on the 15th of November, stated "I have nothing to do with money matters".(Among Edmunds' testimony were details of the opening of the Office in 1852: he was told to engage clerks and "a vast quantity of applications were sent in".)

According to the officially published account, after Greenwood's report Edmunds offered to resign[7], but decided to carry on when he found he could not get a full pension.

In the late summer and autumn of 1863 the breach between Edmunds and Woodcroft became acrimonious and irreparable. In August Edmunds ordered that all requests to the Stationery Office[8] and Office of Works for supplies must be signed by Ruscoe and himself. He also changed the name[9] of the Office on its seal (or more probably heading stamp) from "Office of the Commissioners of Patents..." to "Her Majesty's Patent

Office". He changed the stationery, altering the envelopes, which were printed, "All Correspondence to be Addressed to the Superintendent of Specifications", a direct provocation to Woodcroft. The head of the Stationery Office[10], the economist J.R. McCulloch, refused supplies. Woodcroft appealed to the Commissioners and warned McCulloch of his responsibility if work was held up. The Chancellor tried to mediate.

On the 4th of November, Woodcroft sent a substantial dossier of charges[11] against Edmunds to the Master of the Rolls, Romilly, enclosing copies:

> I am again under the painful necessity of bringing to the notice of your Honour the present state of the Specification Division and of the Patent Museum resulting from Mr Edmunds' assumption of the power of making rules and regulations which under the Act belong only to the Commissioners. It is much to be regretted that Mr Edmunds, who has never given the slightest assistance in the working of this department should have such power to arrest its usefulness.

He complained of interference in the running of the Museum:

> The instructions respecting the Patent Museum appear to me more extraordinary than the rest, inasmuch as neither Mr Edmunds nor Mr Ruscoe have any appointment in the Museum, nor have they either of them at any time obtained a book, a drawing, a portrait, a machine or a model for the Museum or attempted to do so.

From December 1863 to March 1864 Edmunds and Woodcroft exchanged charges and counter charges via the Lord Chancellor, often in the form of marginal comments. The series culminated on the 10th of March when Edmunds dispatched his *First Report of the Clerk of the Patents*[12] in answer to the several statements and allegations in a letter to the Master of the Rolls..." a dossier of over fifty pages, accusing Woodcroft of overspending on correspondence, mismanagement of *The Patent Journal*, irregularities and "jobbery" in connection with the abridgments, including employing his younger brother Zenus and then overpaying his replacement. In an earlier memo he charged Woodcroft with being behind articles in the press and of seeking funds for the Library behind his back.

Edmunds' excited tone lends credence to accounts of his "intemperate" behaviour to the staff. As regards Library supplies:

> Failing with Mr McCulloch he lay bye (sic) for some time, then tried his hand with me. At that time I had heard nothing of the transaction or of his application to Mr McCulloch. He asked me to obtain the money from the Treasury, I refused altogether as peremptorily as Mr McCulloch had before....This is the head and front of my offence – this is the real grievance.

He claimed there was a conspiracy to oust him (which may not have been entirely imaginary). Of the press articles, he wrote:

> No human being can doubt for one moment that they were got up in Woodcroft's office. There is a low grab cabal (sic) or conspiracy in his office, he being the prime mover to get rid of my control and he would be very glad to set up an independent Office for himself, in which to revel in jobs.

Edmunds presented his division as a model of economy and orderliness, in contrast to the undisciplined Specification division. His comments confirm this failure to appreciate its work of which Woodcroft had accused him:

> Woodcroft has no function whatever in the passing of the patents, from the first application to the expiry....He has no custody of any record or instrument.

Woodcroft made a passionate defence[13] of his brother's competence to abridge textile specifications, incidentally throwing light on an otherwise unknown member of the family. Zenus was an invalid:

> My brother was unsurpassed in all the qualifications required for making the abridgments of Cotton Spinning machinery. On leaving school he went through a course of Study such as I never knew a Master Spinner do before or since; he worked for years at the same machines used in a spinning factory, to become a Master.

Zenus had been medically advised to do the abridgments, until Woodcroft was told he was mortally ill and the work was given to an abridger called Brierly. It was in this document that Woodcroft wrote: "There is nothing that would give more satisfaction to myself and the other officers than to have some gentleman appointed by the Commissioners or the Lords of the Treasury to attend and see the working of the Office". This wish was soon to be granted.

On the 16th of March Edmunds sent his *Second Report of the Clerk of the Patents*[14], in refutation of the assertion that the Office is now in a condition of disorganisation"; it included "duties of the several clerks in the Specification Division as defined and lately regulated by me" – a list of the staff with the duties of each in the various sections. Whether wholly accurate or not it is of some interest from the biographical and historical aspect. (How it can be squared with the later charges that Edmunds was absent from the Office for as much as six months a year is a puzzle.) This is the document in which he "courts and requires" (in legal style his verbs often came in pairs) the fullest investigation of his management. It was a rash demand.

In late April 1864 with the approval of the Treasury, the Chancellor appointed John Greenwood, QC, who had carried out the Smith enquiry, and W.M. Hindmarch, QC, a well known patent expert (having decided on "persons of rather high professional grade"). They were offered a fee of 100 guineas and expenses, and instructed to "inquire into the charges against Mr Edmunds and into those against Mr Woodcroft".

The enquiry began at the Patent Office on the 1st of June, 1864. For the first three days Greenwood took notes, as in the Smith enquiry, on the fourth, the 15th of June, an official writer kept a verbatim record. For an official enquiry – what has in more recent cases been called a tribunal – it was unusual in several ways. It was held in the first few days as an open forum, "all the parties indiscriminately taking part in the conversation". Woodcroft and Edmunds the adversaries did not have a full record of the respective charges against them, so there were constant heated demands for papers. Though the inquisitors made a show of impartiality, one suspects that they had decided against Edmunds from the beginning. He did not help his position by being an irascible and uncooperative witness. Woodcroft was permitted to hand in further written accusations that were not shown to Edmunds. While this enquiry was proceeding, on the 7th and 10th of June, Edmunds was a respected witness at the Library and Museum enquiry. (See Ch.9).

The enquiry soon began to reveal a state of affairs that has passed into Civil Service history as an example of the bad old days before public accounts were audited. It dropped its original brief of investigating the charges on both sides and became instead an investigation of Edmunds' and Ruscoe's handling of public money. They first unguardedly disclosed their practice of obtaining stamps for patent documents and sales of documents from the Stamp Office at a discount, selling them to patentees at face value, and keeping the difference. This was the least heinous (some thought entirely legitimate) practice discovered. Edmunds kept the two now notorious accounts at his bank, Coutts, one a "Patent Office Account", the other his private account, and moved money from one to the other as he pleased. The Patent Office Account held the fees still paid for non-invention patents and other monies such as the Treasury grant for running the Commissioners' office. Beginning in 1833 when he became Clerk of the Patents he had, as required by law, made annual payments to the Exchequer but had ceased and allowed the money to accumulate soon after the new Patent Office opened. In 1853 he drew £500 from this account (when stamps replaced fees for invention patents) for Ruscoe's use; when the latter paid it back ten years later it went into his private account. It was hastily repaid into the other one when the enquiry opened. The two had developed other sources of income such as making a little on the tin boxes supplied for impressions of the Great Seal. Another practice they were accused of was making a profit of 12s 6d on each skin of parchment used for the patent grants. It was the continuation of practices, earlier tolerated, when they were well paid salaried officers that was objected to. A third bank account which became subject of enquiry was "Tom's account" belonging to Ruscoe's uncle, the stationer who made a profit on each "folio" copied by the writers he supplied.

The first stage of the enquiry lasted until the 5th of July, 1864, but resumed in November after the long vacation and continued until Christmas. The investigation of accounts to establish Edmunds' liabilities continued for many months. He, however, fled the enquiry after only six days, on the 17th of June.

On the 24th of June the Chancellor was surprised[15] to be visited by Edmunds "in great anxiety", requesting to be allowed to resign his Patent Office posts. The former refused to sign his petition to the Treasury for a pension until the Master of the Rolls, Romilly, had seen it. Eventually he forwarded it to the Treasury, only to recall it when Greenwood came to him urgently, saying that "circumstances of a very fearful character"[16] had arisen.

On the 15th of July Greenwood and Hindmarch sent him their *Preliminary Report*. Edmunds was summoned to appear before the Chancellor and Vice-Chancellor to show why he should not be dismissed from his post as Clerk of the Patents. From this time he ceased to have direct contact with the Chancellor, allowing his solicitor Leman – who found the report "very highly coloured against him"[17]– to mediate on his behalf. William Brougham, Lord Brougham's brother and heir to the title, also took a hand.[18] He was in charge of Lord Brougham's affairs; he knew Edmunds well, and was involved in financial arrangements with him of a very curious kind as will be seen.

After undertaking to pay in to the Treasury all sums due, Edmunds was allowed to resign[19] his Patent Office posts and avoid examination and dismissal. This decision was taken by the Chancellor after consulting the other Patent Commissioners. The Clerkship of the Patents had to be filled, and the Chancellor appointed C.B. Cardew[20] – his son-in-law. Woodcroft became acting Clerk of the Commissioners.[21]

The unfortunate Ruscoe, who had been accused with Edmunds, was suspended at the end of the year and finally dismissed in 1865. The old spirit of Chancery was not exorcised so easily. In May 1865 Hindmarch and Greenwood sent a troubled note[22] to the Chancellor: "though excluded from the building he has continued to the present day to perform elsewhere all the duties of the Clerk of the Patents for Mr Cardew".

The Chancellor now faced the problem of his duty regarding Edmunds' posts in the House of Lords. He had sent a copy of the *Preliminary Report* to two senior law lords, Cranworth and Kingsdown for their opinion. They both held that if the charges were justified, Edmunds could no longer remain[23] an officer of the House.

Both of Edmunds' advisers, though sometimes out of step in their approaches to the Chancellor, urged resignation[24]. Brougham had reasons for avoiding further investigation and obtained the Chancellor's assurance[25] that if "he thinks proper to resign, I will do all that I can with propriety to obtain for him a pension" there being nothing against his conduct in the Lords.

The Chancellor believed that he had this power, but found that it belonged to a Parliament Office Committee (showing an ignorance of procedure not uncommon in holders of high but party office). He consulted other members of the Government who agreed with the law lords that his duty was to make known the charges, to be considered by a Select Committee.

Instead he presented Edmunds, via his advisers, with an ultimatum[26]: unless his petition to be allowed to resign was in the Chancellor's hands by the sitting of the Lords on the 14th of February 1865, he would "move for the Committee and lay the reports on the table". He received it "just as he was taking his seat on the Woolsack" and presented it to the House. It was considered by the *ad hoc* Office Committee appointed each session (called the Committee on the Office of Clerk of the Parliaments and Gentleman Usher of the Black Rod). On the 17th of February the Chancellor moved that the House approve the appointment of the Hon. Slingsby Bethell[27] to the Office of Reading Clerk "in the room of Leonard Edmunds, resigned". Bethell was the Chancellor's second son. Deliberations of the Office Committee were not reported but by the end of February it was known to the press that Edmunds had been granted a pension of £800.

His resignation from the Patent Office and the reason for it were now common knowledge in government and legal circles. He belonged to several West End clubs and had begun to complain at the injustice, as he saw it, of the Hindmarch and Greenwood enquiry. In late February the story of his pension and the Chancellor's new appointment began to be the Victorian equivalent of front page news. It was convenient ammunition for the Conservatives to use against Palmerston's Whig government. *The Morning Star*[28] summed up the criticism of the Chancellor:

> Did the Lord Chancellor press for the retirement of Mr Edmunds?
> Did he do so on the grounds that the suspicions hanging over Mr
> Edmunds rendered him an unsuitable person to hold office under
> the House of Lords? But if this were so, how came the Chancellor to
> play even a passive part in the little farce about the resignation caused

by advancing years? And if the Chancellor himself had compelled the retirement, and believed himself bound in public duty to compel it, how came he to sanction the granting of a pension... ?

Reynold's Newspaper commented: "Lord Westbury's nepotism is, we regret to say. becoming a public scandal. The Bankruptcy and Chancery courts swarm with Bethell's, and whenever a hole is made by death or removal of office, the Lord Chancellor has a Bethell-plug ever ready to stop it with". *The Times* held that "A pension is a reward not for service only, but, as everybody knows, for good and faithful service"[29].

The Chancellor himself was compelled to introduce a debate in the Lords on the 7th of March. Like the eminent lawyer he was, he gave a detailed account of the office of Clerk of the Patents, and how Edmunds came to be appointed to the Commissioners' Office, and the circumstances leading to the grant of the pension. His case was that as Edmunds had a clean record in the Lords and apart from disputed sums, had undertaken to repay the Exchequer, he saw no reason to deprive a long-serving Chancery officer of his pension.

> The Earl of Derby[30] summed up the dissatisfaction with the Chancellor:...The House of Lords should have decided, not whether Mr Edmunds ought to get a pension, but whether he ought to be dismissed. I complain that this question was never submitted.

The Chancellor moved for the appointment of a Select Committee and its members were named on the 9th of March. The case of one patent clerk was now to be considered by a committee chaired by the Lord President, the Earl of Granville, and including a former Prime Minister, the Earl of Derby; Lord Stanley, the Secretary for India; the Duke of Somerset and a former Chancellor, Lord Chelmsford, one of the original Patent Commissioners.

The Committee sat from the 16th of March, 1865 to the 7th of April, examining Edmunds himself, the Chancellor, the Master of the Rolls, the solicitor Leman, William Brougham, Greenwood, Ruscoe, Treasury officials and Gladstone, the Chancellor of the Exchequer. It sat in camera but as each day's disclosures became known outside, public appetite for news of the "scandal" was supplied by leaders in the serious press and cartoons, squibs and lampoons in satirical journals.

Its report, issued to Parliament on the 4th of May found three of the charges[31] against Edmunds, of having improperly taken discounts, of withholding large sums due to the Exchequer and of transferring public money for his private use fully proved. On a fourth, of having deliberately withheld part of the Smith money for himself, he was given the benefit of the doubt. The Committee criticised the Chancellor for keeping the Office Committee in the dark as to the circumstances of Edmunds' resignation leaving it "with no clearer light than that which could be derived from vague and uncertain rumours". But it did not spare that Committee itself for not acting "upon their general knowledge or impression so far as to interpose some delay" before granting the pension.

In his evidence the Chancellor of the Exchequer, Gladstone, had made some remarkable admissions as to the lack of accountability of the Clerk of the Patents, who "may hold in his hands just as much money as he thinks fit, and pay it if he thinks fit, and if he pay nothing at all there are no means of calling him to account". (The situation did not weigh heavily on the Chancellor of the Exchequer judging by the laconic entry in his diary[32], "Examined before the Edmunds Committee" followed by a dinner appointment.) This was to some degree in Edmunds' favour: the Committee commented that such a situation "offers to various persons temptation to misconduct". The Report is remarkable for its lucidity and forensic grasp of the issues, comparing rather well with, say, the Scott report into arms for Iraq of the 1980s.

The Committee also considered it was its duty to "advert" to the circumstances of Edmunds' first appointment[33] as Clerk of the Patents in 1833. As revealed in the examination of Edmunds himself, of William Brougham and Leman, very interesting they proved to be, modifying any simple black-and-white view of his case.

In 1811 the Broughams had borrowed £5,000 by mortgaging one of their northern properties. Henry Peter Brougham, the future Chancellor, was party to the agreement. In 1827 the mortgage had to be paid off and they borrowed the necessary £5,000 from Edmunds' father's estate. The mortgage was assigned to an Edmunds family trust, the £200 annual interest to go to his two sisters.

When Edmunds was appointed in 1833 it was agreed with James Brougham, another brother, that £300 of his salary of £400 should go to the Broughams, £200 to pay the mortgage interest and £100 to the family of another brother, John Brougham. Edmunds was thus working largely to pay interest due to his own family.

Circumstances revealed by the enquiry unfolded like a Victorian novel. In 1834 William Brougham took over the family affairs on the death of his brother and the arrangement continued. In 1840, William insured Edmunds' life for £3,000 against the ceasing of his salary and the mortgage having to be paid off. Then in 1845 he borrowed £1,200 from Edmunds, paying no interest directly, but merely reducing the amount he received from Edmunds' salary (intended for John Brougham's family) using the balance for the insurance premium.

In 1863 Edmunds had approached Brougham to formalise their financial arrangements regarding the paying off of the mortgage and the loan. Brougham then wrote him in tones recalling George Eliot's grandee Grandcourt (in *Daniel Deronda*) to his agent: "my dear Leonard, I am sorry you propose to die, but take care not to do so till I get back, and we will then arrange the best way to state the account". His evasiveness was exposed during the enquiry; in spite of his denial of knowledge of the arrangement concerning Edmunds' salary he had planned to replace Edmunds by his own son had the former resigned in 1863. Edmunds was to "take care to be in the same story with me" i.e. that part of the salary was committed. The Report commented[34], "Any private arrangement that a portion of the salary of a public officer that is a remuneration for his services shall be applied to the benefit of any other person is a grave offence against public morality". Affronted Victorian morality as expressed by the press could now add the misdeeds of the great and good to the scandal of a clerk and his pension. Edmunds' position had a new dimension, in some quarters he was "Mr Worthyman", opposed to "William Basegreed, Lord Screwham". The Lords were relieved to be able to absolve Lord Brougham himself from all blame; from Cannes he sent vehement affidavits denying all knowledge of the arrangements. He was still a revered figure.

The Report was debated in the Lords on the 9th of May. Edmunds was refused a hearing in his own defence and on a motion by Earl Granville he was deprived[35] of his pension. (*The Times* devoted some 150 column-inches to the debate.) Considerably later, because other reports concerning the Lord Chancellor's appointments were pending, on July 3rd there was a vote of censure on him in the Commons and he resigned. In addition to charges of nepotism, his severity toward other officers was contrasted with his leniency to Edmunds. The Chancellor was liked but his supporters were unable to help. Gladstone confided[36] to his diary, "We discussed the terrible Westbury matter (in cabinet) and whether to do more on it. The Westbury affair occupied me much".

Edmunds was ruined, but his case was far from closed. The Hindmarch and Greenwood enquiry had concluded (with the accountancy help of the Patent Museum clerk, Pemberton Gipps who was paid a fee[37]) that Edmunds still owed the Exchequer a large sum. Their *Final Report* again condemned him but glowed with praise of Woodcroft and his staff. After the generation of an immoderate amount of documentation[38] by the Treasury and the Law Officers as to how to proceed, Edmunds dropped a counter action in return for arbitration. It was decided he still owed more than £7,000. In 1869 the Treasury published a minute[39] stating its own case which Edmunds considered libellous and he started his own proceedings against the Prime Minister, Gladstone, and the Treasury Commissioners. In May, 1870 a detective was hired[40] to find where he was living. He was arrested for debt "at the suit of the Crown" and was committed to the Whitecross St[41] prison, in his own words, from the 12th of June to the 25th of January, 1871. He claimed that Greenwood ordered his release to avoid a warrant from the Speaker.

In 1872 and again in 1873 Lord Redesdale[42] proposed a motion for a re-audit of Edmunds' accounts by the new Comptroller and Auditor General whose office (established 1866) was partly an outcome of the case but it was rejected. Another sympathiser, Lord Rosebery[43], sought a new enquiry by the Office Committee but the Chancellor, Lord Cairns, refused it. Edmunds' action against Gladstone was non-suited. In 1879, as a last throw, Lord Redesdale tried to obtain a re-examination of the case by select committee, but failed. Edmunds' own long account *The History of the Edmunds Scandal* "full of virulent and intemperate accusations[44] against a whole range of public officials" had been reprinted the same year[45] – by the House of Lords.

There is evidence of sympathy for him in an unexpected quarter. In a bundle of papers dated May and June, 1868, including a letter from Edmunds to Disraeli, there is a note from 11 Downing St[46], probably from Disraeli himself:

I think the right course is for the a/c to be taken according to the rule of the Vice-Chancellor. Should the result show that Mr Edmunds has been a loser by, or not sufficiently remunerated for the discharge of his duties as Clerk of the Patents, the Govt. ought to consider the matter in a liberal spirit toward Mr Edmunds.

In 1885 the House of Lords awarded Edmunds a compassionate allowance[47] of £2.10s a week, until his death in 1887.

His case is beset with ambiguities. One of his successors in the Lords in this century has recorded a charitable last word[48]:

Edmunds' case was a sad one. He was a man of uneven temper and poor judgement, at least where his own affairs were concerned. His violence of language and extreme partisanship obviously lost him the sympathy of the officials who had to deal with his problems. On the other hand, while it is impossible to defend his conduct over the affairs of the Patent Office, it is only fair to say that Edmunds was to some extent a victim of the changing morality of the Victorian era.

Notes to Chapter 8

1	he laid off eight clerks	Woodcroft to Fitzroy Kelly, 27.7. 1859, PRO TS 18-536.
2	a heated justification	Ibid, do, 1.8.1859 (copy, in Woodcroft to Master of the Rolls, 4.11.1863.)
3	Smith was suspended	Patent Office, Staff Register.
4	an anonymous tip-off	John Greenwood. Enquiry, "Statements of Officers", PRO TS18-536.
5	offered to make out a list	Patent Office, Staff Register.
6	report of the Treasury Solicitor	Greenwood to the Commissioners of Patents, 2.1.1863, PRO TS18-536.
7	Edmunds offered to resign	Lords Committee on the Resignation of certain Offices, Report, 1865. p.iii.
8	Edmunds ordered that all requests	E. to Ruscoe, 8.8.1863, (copy in Woodcroft to MR, 4.11.1863.) TS18-536.
9	changed the name	Ibid, Woodcroft to MR, as cited.(Specimen envelope enclosed.)
10	Stationery Office refused supplies	Ibid, McCulloch to Woodcroft, 8.12.1863. TS18-536.

11 dossier of charges   Ibid, Woodcroft to MR, as cited.

12 Edmunds despatched his   Ibid, E. to the Commissioners, 10.3. 1864.
First Report

13 Woodcroft made a   Ibid, *Statement by Mr B.W. to the Clerk of the Patents*,
passionate defence   30.1.1864. (Copy, in Edmunds' *First Report*, 10.3.1864.)

14 *Second Report of the Clerk*   Ibid, Edmunds to Commissioners of Patents, 16.3.1864.

15 the Chancellor was   Lords' Committee, 1865, as cited, Report p.iv.
surprised

16 circumstances of a very   Ibid, p.iv.
fearful character

17 "very highly coloured   Ibid, p.iv.
against him"

18 William Brougham...   Ibid, p.xi, xii.
also took a hand

19 Edmunds was allowed to   Ibid, p.v.
resign

20 the Chancellor appointed   Ibid, Minutes, 24.3.1865. Chancellor's evidence.
C.B. Cardew

21 Woodcroft became   Ibid.
acting Clerk of the
Commissioners

22 a troubled note   Hindmarch & Greenwood to Chancellor, 5.5.1865,
PRO TS18-536.

23 Edmunds could no   Lords Committee, Report, p.x (Lord Kingsdown to
longer remain   Chancellor, 8.8.1864.).

24 Edmunds' advisers ...   Ibid, Chancellor to Master of the Rolls. 29.7.1864;
urged resignation   10.11.1864.

25 obtained the Chancellor's   Ibid, Chancellor to Wm Brougham, 29.10.1864,
assurance   Minutes, Chancellor's evidence, 24.3.1865.

26 presented Edmunds...   Ibid, Report, p.xiii.
with an ultimatum

27 appointment of S. Bethell   *The Morning Star*, 27.2.1865 (Ex *Hansard*).

28 *The Morning Star*   7.3.1865.
summed up

29 *The Times* held that   7.3.1865.
a pension

30 The Earl of Derby   in the Lords, 7.3.1865. (*The Times*, 8.3. 1865.)

31 three of the charges   Lords Committee, Report, p.v–vii.

32 laconic entry in his diary for 27.3.1865, *The Gladstone Diaries* ed. HCG Mathews. Oxford, 1978.Vol.6, p.344.

33 circumstances of E's first   Lords Committee, Report, p.xiv–xviii.
    appointment

34 The Report commented p.xviii.

35 he was deprived   *The Times*, Parliamentary Intelligence, 10.5.1865.

36 Gladstone confided   *Diaries*, vol 6, as cited p.366.

37 Gipps, who was paid a fee Treasury letter, 9.7.1867, PRO TS18-536.

38 immoderate   the bulk of PRO TS18-536 is evidence enough.
    documentation

39 Treasury published a   dated 14.12.1869, Ibid.
    minute

40 a detective was hired Memo to Assistant Solicitor, 31.5.1870, PRO as cited.

41 was committed to   Affidavit from Edmunds, 14.11. 1971, PRO as cited.
    Whitecross St

42 Lord Redesdale   Sainty, *The Edmunds Case*, p.63.

43 Lord Rosebery   Ibid.

44 full of virulent   Ibid, p.63.
    accusations

45 reprinted the same year Ibid.

46 a note from 11   24.6.1868, PRO TS18-536.
    Downing St

47 a compassionate   Sainty (citing the Lords *Journal*), 117 p.68.
    allowance

48 a charitable last word Ibid.

9 Ten years – three enquiries, 1862-72

The effect of the Edmunds affair on public auditing and accounting was greater than on the Office itself where – as Harding has pointed out – work continued much as before, confirming the view of Woodcroft and his staff that he was irrelevant. The only permanent Commissioner, the Master of the Rolls, and the Treasury kept a closer eye on it[1] than before – surprising if they had not, in view of the unwanted publicity.

The novelty and enthusiastic early reception of the Office did not last. As the working of the 1852 Act became clearer there were complaints about the large number of patents being granted for trivial, old or useless inventions, as a result of the facility and diminished cost of obtaining them. There were complaints too at the potentially huge cost of litigating patent cases. The only real patent examiners were expert witnesses and expensive counsel, in the courts.

There was now intense pressure for further reform; the Commissioners received many petitions from groups in the industrial towns; special committees of the British Association for the Advancement of Science, the Society of Arts and various inventors' associations produced draft legislation. Many engineers, industrialists, patent agents and lawyers used the popular medium of the pamphlet to put forward their views. These middle years of Victoria's reign were the last of Britain's indisputable world dominance in industry and there was some realisation of the fact. The number of patents granted rose steadily, almost doubling between 1860 and 1883. During this period of growth, aniline dyes, Bessemer steel, the dynamo, sewing machine, electric light, phonograph and telephone were all introduced, with many other significant inventions largely invisible to those who benefit from them. Patents had an understandably high profile. Abolitionists still existed, but orthodox opinion backed up by the economists was in favour.[2]

The ten years 1862-72 saw two important enquiries into patent law, by Royal Commission and Commons Select Committee respectively and a third into the Library and Museum. The law enquiries had no immediate result, but the second prepared the ground for the legislation of 1883.

The first of the three enquiries of this decade to report was the Commons Select Committee on the Patent Office Library and Museum (July 19, 1864). Its mover in Parliament and chairman was Lewis Llewelyn Dillwyn (1814-1892), proprietor of the Cambrian Pottery and MP for Swansea. He had been a watchdog[3] of the Patent Office, asking awkward questions about costs and duties. From the human aspect it is striking that during these hearings of early June Edmunds was competently answering questions while his world was collapsing about him in the internal enquiry that ran parallel. The hostility between him and Woodcroft is however evident.

The other principal witnesses were the engineers Joseph Bazalgette, William Fairbairn and E.R. Cowper, the lawyer Thomas Webster, and Henry Cole and Pettit Smith from the South Kensington and Patent Museums respectively. Apart from the particular function of a Patent Museum, much of interest concerning scientific or technical museums emerged. The Report proposed the dual concept[4] of a Museum of Mechanical Inventions, the best of ancient and modern as in the present Science Museum, with a models-only Patent Museum as a possible extra.

The enquiry had been dominated by the single question of proper accommodation and the Report called in the strongest terms[5] for the adoption of a suitable site for a new Patent Office and Library.

The question of a proper Patent Office and where to build it had been current for years. It was thought scandalous that an Office generating such huge surplus revenue should still be confined to the wretched, dingy, cramped Masters' Offices. In 1857 the journal *The Engineer* had published[6] a provocative feature showing the American Patent Office juxtaposed with a ground plan of the pygmy Southampton Buildings site. (Incidentally interesting as the only record until the relevant plans if any are found in the Works files at the Record Office.)

The Patent Commissioners, well plied with data from Woodcroft and his colleagues, published a plea to the Treasury[7] in their 1858 Report citing the pressures on the Library particularly. The latter was held in special regard – "unique" according to *The Engineer*. In 1859 (1860) in another plea to the Treasury they reported that a site had been found[8], part of the then garden of Burlington House. Plans had been prepared by the important and prolific government architect James (later Sir James)

Pennethorne (1801-1871) and submitted to the Minister of Works. Then Derby's second administration was replaced by Palmerston's and the scheme was dropped. In their Report of August, 1862, the Commissioners of Patents proposed the site of the early 19th century Fife House near the Thames on the route of a planned new road (now Horse Guards Avenue) running from the planned Embankment to Whitehall. The proposal was accompanied by a petition from R.W. Kennard, MP and others[9]. In early 1863 Pennethorne submitted bold plans[10] for a Patent Office and Museum, to cost £100, 000. There were delays with the Embankment plans, and this too came to nothing. The Commissioners repeated their now rather pathetic appeals to the Treasury.

Other sites discussed were on Victoria Street, at South Kensington and on the north side of Trafalgar Square. This last was to occupy ground behind Wilkins' National Gallery after the demolition of a workhouse (St Martin's) and other buildings. There was some utopianism; one correspondent to *The Engineer* envisaged a super Patent Office here, combining a library and information centre to serve all possible needs of art and industry and joined by learned societies. The engineer and consultant E.A. Cowper tendered to the enquiry a detailed architect's brief[11] with every workspace defined, and a bookstore basement with delivery by hydraulic lift. Another contributor produced an analysis of the distance of each site from legal and other institutions. Pennethorne proposed using a slum district east of Chancery Lane and north of his own Record Office.

The site favoured by the Committee[12] and probably by far the best, on traditional Chancery ground and in the legal heartland of London, was adjacent to and behind Southampton Buildings in a large area bounded by Chancery Lane, Cursitor Street to the south and Took's Court to the east. It would have been larger than the Office built at the end of the century. It was proposed by the Inventor's Institute which produced coloured plans[13] and formed a company, The Inventor's Association Ltd[14], with a capital of £10,000; a private finance initiative seems to have been intended.

The Committee's Report had no outcome in a new Patent Office, but with the larger scheme in abeyance the case for relieving the Library was stronger than ever. In 1866, Pennethorne was briefed[15] to convert the upper floor and roof space of the Masters' offices into a new Library. (See Ch.14.)

Harding's account[16] of the two law enquiries is impeccable and a writer now can do little but quote or paraphrase it. The 1862-4 Royal Commission was moved in Parliament by Sir Hugh Cairns, MP for Belfast, who had been a Patent Commissioner and would be again as Lord Chancellor. It was chaired by Lord Stanley, son and heir of the Earl of Derby. Its membership included the lawyers W.M. Hindmarch (one of the QCs investigating the Office in 1864) and W.R. Grove. Engineering was represented by William Fairbairn, John Scott Russell and Sir William Armstrong. Besides Woodcroft and Edmunds, those examined included Thomas Webster.

This enquiry and its report (July 1865) are striking evidence of Victorian official style; in addition to oral evidence questions were circulated to many regional bodies such as Chambers of Commerce, to reform associations and the special committees of bodies such as the British Association. Woodcroft was asked to check the first 100 patents granted in certain years and found that up to a quarter were bad from want of novelty.

There was great diversity of views, on fees, duration of a patent and its possible extension, and on the mode of examination. Armstrong and Scott Russell were sceptical of the value of the system as a whole. Service chiefs described the way opportunists would take out patents for systems already in wide use, such as armour plate in wooden ships, and then sue for infringement or threaten to. Webster repeated his strong views[17] on the function of the Law Officers:

> Do you think that the enquiry which takes place before the Law Officers is sufficient or satisfactory? —I think that it is not only useless but positively mischievous in many ways ... first of all you have two Law Officers and they have no way of knowing that the one may not be granting a patent for the same thing as the other, practically everything is patented, and under a show of examination there is practically none.

The report was unsatisfactory; a critic in *The Westminster Review*[18] suggested that the Commission was unable to agree. It had failed to grasp the need for professional examiners, recommending instead the retention of the Law Officers, to be aided by a board of barristers and scientists. On less important matters it was forthright but wrong, in, for instance, ruling out extensions of the patent term, an established but rare practice.

On the question of litigation in patent disputes the Commission recommended a non-specialist judge backed up by scientists, with no jury. In an important supplementary report, Hindmarch, an expert[19], recommended that the grant should depend on a "clear and distinct statement of claim or claims" in the specification and that this should be approved by "competent persons appointed for that purpose". Here he envisaged a cornerstone of the system as it evolved. He proposed a register of patent agents, to end some of the improper practices revealed in the evidence. The main report concluded that a perfect system was impossible, and the imperfections were the price to be paid for having a system at all.

This rather half-hearted – and with the exception of Hindmarch's – unspecific set of findings had no outcome and the Commissioners of Patents continued to receive petitions, some of them in a wider reform context. In 1866 a special committee[20] of two of the many Victorian improvement societies, for Social Science and Law Amendment submitted proposals exemplifying the gradual acceptance of the role of examining officers:

> Provisional protection should only be granted upon the certificate of an examining officer: that competent examining officers should report on novelty, subject matter and the sufficiency of the provisional specification; that oppositions should be heard by the examining officers; that appeals should be to the Law Officer; that no proceedings should be commenced except upon the certificate of the examining officer; that in any court proceedings it should be competent for the judge to refer any application to the examining officer and that any obstructiveness on the part of the patentee should be met by compulsory licences.

In 1868 the Manchester Patent Law Reform Committee[21] recalled the Royal Commission's recommendation that "an enquiry as to novelty sufficient to avoid the grant of successive patents for the same invention should be made and called for the appointment of commissioners to

81

represent 'mechanical, chemical and natural science' of whom the representative of natural science should also be 'a person of legal knowledge and specially conversant with the patent system' ".

The high profile of patents at this time is evident from the appointment of a Commons Select Committee to hold the second major enquiry[22] within a few years. Chaired by Bernhard Samuelson, MP for Banbury and an industrialist prominent in technical education, it heard evidence during the summer of 1871 and the spring of 1872. The witnesses included lawyers, patent agents, inventors, manufacturers and officials. In addition to Woodcroft, there was the refreshing inclusion of a clerk, the hard-worked W. Marwick Michell. Its findings, in two more analytical volumes were important, but far from unanimous:

> The lawyers were curiously pessimistic[23], for Mr Grove, QC, FRS, a famous patent lawyer and member of the Royal Commission of 1862, Lord Romilly, who had been Master of the Rolls and a Patent Commissioner from the first, and Sir Roundell Palmer, a law officer for six years were all in favour of abolishing the law of patents unless it could be improved, which they doubted. Sir William Armstrong the engineer was of the same opinion, but the majority of engineers such as Bessemer, Nasmyth and Siemens were strongly in favour as were many industrialists such as the President of the Birmingham Chamber of Commerce, Mr Wright, who informed the Committee that 'the manufacturers, almost to a man, are in favour of patents, and the working men are, as a rule, in favour'.

It was difficult to ignore such testimony as that of C.W. Siemens[24], who had come to England as representative of the Berlin firm Siemens und Halske, was now founder of the English branch and one of the "makers of the modern world". He stated that it was the patent system that decided him to settle in this country.

Woodcroft's evidence[25] was obviously important but not for the first time he was out of step with progress. "He contended for instance, that every patentee should make his own searches and prepare his own abridgments; he was against preliminary examination and preferred to leave the public to take care of itself". Signs of impatience[26] on the Committee's side provoked some testiness on his. (One recalls his age and recurring ill-health.)

The report contained the first statement from a Government-appointed body of important principles:

> The subsequent history[27] of the patent system and the Patent Office is mainly concerned with the implementation of these principles. The Committee found that patents stimulated the rapid introduction of important inventions and a large number of minor ones; that they should only be granted on a clear description of the alleged points of novelty and after report of a competent authority that the invention was properly patentable; that specifications should be thrown open to inspection prior to the grant to facilitate opposition; that the patent should be conditional on the supply of the manufactured article on reasonable terms; that patent fees should be low and earmarked for Patent Office administration; that patent trials should be before a judge with skilled technical assistance; that the Commissioners should be reinforced by persons of legal scientific and technical experience; that reciprocal arrangements with foreign countries should be instituted and that improved indexes and abridgments should be prepared.

It would be more than ten years before implementation began.

Notes to Chapter 9

1 kept a closer eye on it — the earliest entry in a MS volume of *Commissioners Instructions* is for 1876. BLSRIS SC.

2 orthodox opinion...was in favour — "by about 1875 the tide of opinion was beginning to change" – Harding, p.24
"he did not think it necessary to argue at any length in favour of a Patent Law.. there had been a very great change of opinion..." – Joseph Chamberlain in the Commons, 1883.

3 L.L. Dillwyn, a watchdog — e.g. his Commons order for a return of Office expenses, 8.7.1863.

4 The Report proposed the dual concept — Select Committee on the Patent Office Library and Museum. Report, p.iv.

5 called in the strongest terms — Ibid, p.iii.

6 *The Engineer* had published — 31.7.1857, p.76.

7 a plea to the Treasury — Commissioners' Report, 1858, pp.4-7.

8   a site had been found   Ibid, 1859, p.7.

9   a petition from R.W.   Ibid, 1862, p.8.

10 Pennethorne submitted   Tyack, Geoffrey, *Sir James Pennethorne and the Making of*
    bold plans   *Victorian London*, CUP 1992, p.276.

11 a detailed architect's brief Select Committee as cited, App.5, p.143.

12 The site favoured by the   Ibid, Report, p.vi.
    Committee

13 produced coloured plans   example in BLSRIS SC.

14 The Inventors'   Select Committee, as cited, Webster's evidence Q. 1572-
    Association   4; Richardson, R., Q.1663-4.

15 Pennethorne was briefed   Tyack, as cited, p.276.

16 Harding's account   Patent Office Centenary, pp.14-16; 22-24.

17 Webster repeated his   Commissioners Appointed to Enquire into the Working
    strong views   of the Law Relative to Patents for Inventions, Report,
                               1864. Minutes, 26.2.1863, Q.1670.

18 *The Westminster Review*   82, 1864, pp.322-7, *The Patent Laws*.

19 Hindmarch, an expert   Royal Commission Report, p.xv-xvii, 29.9.1864.

20 In 1866 a special   Harding, p.22.
    committee

21 Manchester Patent Law   Select Committee on Letters Patent Report, 1871,
    Reform Committee   App.2, p.200.

22 second major enquiry   Ibid, Report, 1871, 1872.

23 The lawyers' pessimistic   Harding, p.22.

24 testimony of Siemens   Select Committee as cited, 1872, Minutes, 7.3.1872,
                               Q.404.

25 Woodcroft's evidence   Harding, pp.22-23.

26 Signs of impatience   Report, Minutes, 19.3.1872, passim.

27 The subsequent history   Harding, p.23.

1. Bennet Woodcroft as a young man, from a miniature
(National Portrait Gallery and Hugh Carey).

THE PATENT OFFICE
LIBRARY
NOON DAY.

2. Noon Day, 1865, tinted pencil drawing (BLSRIS SC).

3. Settling Day: a Story of the Times. *Lords Westbury and Brougham? The allusion is to a play by Tom Taylor.* From Fun, *April 8, 1865 (BLSRIS SC).*

When Her
Majesty was
asked by the
Lord Mayor
whether she
was pleased
with the City,
she is reported
to have replied
in the ver-
nacular of
the Cockney
Aldermen –
"V.R"!

What is the
difference
between the
Turks and
the Russians?
The one are
'Ottermen the
others are
colder-men.

THE LAST FLICKER OF THE EDMUNDS CANDLE.

Shamus Powell, Sure me dear Leonard was it the "gross miscarriage
of Justice" that has brought ye to this!

4. *The last flicker of the Edmunds candle, from* The Patent Office Almanac, 1870
(BLSRIS SC).

AT THE PATENT OFFICE: THE LIBRARY.

5. *Another view of Pennethorne's Library.*
Drawing from Cassell's Saturday Journal, *c. 1890.*

6. *Pennethorne's Library (BLSRIS SC).*

7. *Richard Bissell Prosser. From an unpublished volume of Patent Office staff caricatures (BLSRIS SC).*

8. Staff asking for their share of the cake? Source as Plate 7.

9. South end of the "Boilers", showing the separate entrance of the Patent Museum. From a watercolour by J.C. Lanchenick (Victoria & Albert Museum).

10. The older Bennet Woodcroft (BLSRIS SC).

SIR HENRY READER LACK.
COMPTROLLER GENERAL.
1884 – 1897.

11. Sir Henry Reader Lack, First Comptroller General (The Patent Office).

10 Designs and trade marks

In 1875 there were significant changes in the Office when the Commissioners' jurisdiction was enlarged by the transfer of the Design Registry from the Board of Trade and the establishment of a Trade Marks Registry. These changes involved links, mainly in the form of staff, with the Board of Trade that were a portent of the future and the end of the Commissioners' regime.

As they reported[1], "The Registry of Designs was transferred from Whitehall to the Patent Office building, 11th March, 1875, and officials of the Designs Office commenced their attendance at the latter place on that day. On the 21st April Mr B. Woodcroft was appointed Registrar of Designs by the Board of Trade". The Registry moved as a functioning office though the Act, the Copyright of Designs Act (38,39 Vict. c. 93) was not passed until the 13th of August and authority did not pass until 1876. (Just where the Registry was put is a mystery, in the already inadequate offices.) The addition of this Registry to Woodcroft's other responsibilities neatly eliminated the separate salaried post under the Board of Trade. The adjacent Trade Marks Registration Act (c.91) for the establishment of a Registry of Trade Marks and their proprietors under the Commissioners was to take effect from January 1, 1876.

Copyright of designs[2] is concerned with protection of intellectual property in the appearance and decoration of manufactured products. It first applied in the last quarter of the 18th century to provide limited protection for the design of printed textiles. (Earlier, such characteristics were occasionally protected by patent.) The introduction of registration in 1839 by the Board of Trade followed a select committee enquiry with an educational brief, and the introduction of registration is contemporaneous with the founding of the national Schools of Design. The 1839 Copyright of Designs Act extended protection generally to "Articles of Manufacture". In this finicky area of intellectual property there were some 14 Acts before 1900 and there have been several since, to keep pace with technical development.

The Registry moving into Southampton Buildings was on a modest scale[3], consisting, under Woodcroft as Registrar, of two clerks, R.D.

Spinks and B. Tall, a printer and two messengers. The Assistant Registrar, J. Lowry Whittle, did not join until April 1876 when he also became Assistant Registrar of Trade Marks. (Woodcroft, though his career was almost over, was an appropriate Registrar in view of his textile background.) The Registry's move was welcomed by the press, *The Engineer* reprinted the approval of *The Times*, which welcomed the possibility of publication and indexing of designs, as with patents.

Quality Court[4] is one of the quainter recesses of legal London; *The Times'* writer's impression of it has been quoted above. No 4 was the last address on the north side; preceding it from the entrance on Chancery Lane were the Office of the Registrar, Office of Appeal in Bankruptcy and Office for Registration of Arraignment Proceedings in Bankruptcy at No 2, and at No 3 the Registrar in Lunacy, both part of the fabric of the Patent Office building and source of the oldest (now rather wearisome) joke about it.

The Trade Marks Registry opened here[5] on January 1st, 1876, to a queue of applicants. No 1 mark to be recorded for registration, appropriately for an ale-drinking nation, was the Bass red triangle; other early marks were those of "T. and J. Colman, Chas. and John Boosey, E. Dent and Co., Callard and Bowser, the Procurator of the Monastery of La Grande Chartreuse, Thomas de la Rue and Thomas Beecham".

The founding staff consisted of two men from the Board of Trade, the Temporary Registrar H. Reader Lack and J.H. Clark. They were joined by two clerks from the Specification Division (W.J. Tomlinson and E.T. Kingsford), two "extra" clerks from the Patent Division (G. Stanford and T.W.H. Davies) another clerk, W.E. Milliken from the Board of Education, five writers and two messengers. J. Lowry Whittle soon took over from Clark as Assistant Registrar of both registries.

Whittle was an MA and barrister[6] who had been a parliamentary draughtsman in the Irish Office; under Lack he was to shape the working and share the buffets of the untried Registry for many years. The character of Lack, the man who kept his niche at the Board of Trade until he could succeed Woodcroft in a few weeks as head of the Office, is still mysterious. In terms of offices and honours his career looks successful, but he was in charge during a time when public dissatisfaction and internal discontent were greatest, culminating in the Herschell enquiry of 1886/7 part of the findings of which were kept secret.

He belonged to a minor dynasty of Lacks[7] who had held offices in the Board of Trade since the late 18th century. Born in 1832, he joined it in 1847; at eighteen he was working for the 1851 Exhibition Commissioners. Described by one writer as born under a lucky star, his luck was certainly backed up by an eye for opportunity. The family expertise was in the field of commercial statistics; his father had been Deputy Comptroller of Corn Returns. He first made his mark assisting Richard Cobden with the groundwork for the important Anglo-French Trade Treaty of 1860[8], a favoured project of Gladstone's. (The son of the Corn Comptroller concerned with the data for applying the Corn Laws, was assisting the Corn Law reformer in promoting free trade.) Lack worked with the Commission in France for months and published a slim explanatory volume[9] on the Treaty, Cobden offered to assist his career but with or without help he rose unspectacularly from 2nd class to senior clerk in the Board. He represented it in Vienna[10] as part of the Anglo-Austrian Tariff Commission and again in 1872 at the International Statistical Congress at St Petersburg. He held office in the Royal Statistical Society and the Society of Arts. At first Lack was only seconded to the Patent Office, indeed it is reported that he accepted the by now surely minimal post of Comptroller of Corn Returns[11] at the same time as becoming Registrar of Trade Marks.

The new Registry was far from universally welcomed. Trade Marks are an elusive[12] and multifarious form of industrial property: they are emblems, devices or words denoting the maker or origin of goods or services. For the customer they are a means of recognition and distinction, hence their value to their owner. The right to trade marks as property did not exist in statute law until 1875, but a right to defend them against fraud, deception and "passing off" had long been recognised in common law and equity and many felt it was enough. However, "until the 1875 Act[13] every plaintiff had first to prove that his mark was distinctive in relation to his goods, for if it was not there could be no trespass upon it. All such cases therefore tended to be lengthy and expensive and by the middle of the 19th century they were cluttering the courts ... the situation was aggravated by the great upsurge in the use of trade marks in the third quarter of the century..."

There had been an attempt to legislate[14] in 1862 but the Select Committee (to which Woodcroft and Edmunds testified) did not recommend the Bill. Registration, by being made equivalent to public use of a mark, would confer a statutory right to existing marks, and a means of search to those wishing to adopt one. It was felt that assignment of a trade mark would deceive the public as to the origin of goods and that registration would be troublesome and expensive to existing users. The case for easier litigation and protection of the public eventually prevailed but fears of problems were justified.

Stress and evident confusion[15] characterised the setting up and first months of the Trade Marks Registry, a period of, in polite terms, teething troubles. Reader Lack did not take up his post until December 1875, only days before the opening. Though the Registry had been announced in the Act, it was not until the 29th December that a hastily inserted notice appeared in *The Times* in response to a reader's complaint, giving its location. The first set of Rules under the Act for the guidance of applicants did not appear until two days before the opening after – as the journal *Engineering* put it – "months of weary waiting", noting that they were five times as long as the Act itself. (The technical press was seldom sympathetic to the practical difficulties of administration.) *Engineering* invoked the shade of the Circumlocution Office, displeased with inadequate access to the indexes, the charges for inspecting the register, and the Registry's refusal to accept coin: "the notion of compelling a person who tenders gold to be at the trouble of procuring a post office order". Had the appointment of a Board of Trade official caused a decline in the liberal service of the Office? Curiously, no use was made at first of the obvious means of communication with the public, *The Patent Journal*. While publishing lists of foreign trademarks and designs (under Woodcroft's exchange arrangements) no mention of the Registry appeared until six months after opening, and this to announce in June 1876 that the *Trade Marks Journal* would start publishing in May.

Codification of trade mark rights by statute aroused widespread opposition[16] especially in the textile industries[17]. Registration was radical in that marks not registered within a time limit of initially six months lost their owner's right to sue for infringement. The textile industries used a huge variety of marks, some distinctive of individual firms but more were common marks used widely for varieties of product or products intended for particular markets, where they were traditionally accepted. It was feared that there would be a race to register formerly common marks. Registration was not three months old when the Manchester Chamber of Commerce, the hastily formed Trade Marks Association and the Bleachers Association petitioned the Commons for amendment of the Rules for certain classes. Two local MPs met the Chancellor, Cairns, and another Manchester deputation met the Registrar. Some Scottish regional associations petitioned for repeal of the Act. The time limit was soon extended, twice by special Acts and once by Order in Council, into 1877 and 1878. Victorian governments did not lightly take on Manchester: in August 1876 new rules provided for a Manchester Branch[18] of the Registry which opened in October. It was to work with a local 20-strong Committee of Experts to consider the 60,000 existing textile marks, dividing them into two classes, of proprietary and "common" marks, a task which lasted until 1879. By an astute stroke the Secretary of the Manchester Trade Marks Association, Mr Joseph Fry, an experienced business man, was appointed to head the new registry as Keeper of Cotton Marks. The official history is not quite truthful in giving the impression that the Manchester branch was planned as part of the original Act. Other trades presented the same difficulty of distinguishing between registrable and common marks, and like textiles were exempted from the operation of the Act. Needle manufacture[19] was one, forming its own committee of experts, headed by the still household name of Millward. The Sheffield Cutlers[20] was another body that had its own traditional arrangements.

Improvised measures such as the brief appearance of Mr Clark from the Board of Trade, the move of several clerks from patents to the new field of trade marks and similar reshuffles cannot have eased the early days of the Registry. In 1880 or 1881 the Chancellor, Lord Cairns, retired Mr Wylde[21], the Registrar (or Master) in Lunacy – a neighbour in Quality Court – and to replace him plucked Mr Lowry Whittle from his post as Assistant Registrar of Designs and Trade Marks putting in his place his own nephew Capt. William Macneile Cairns. As early as May, 1881, the Captain left on a year's sick leave, on full pay it is said. "Nepotism" seems particularly apt, in this instance. The post was filled until February, 1883 by William Marwick Michell[22] who was presumably also Assistant Registrar of Designs. But this is to anticipate.

The several amendments to the original Act, and changes in the Rules, gave an impression that the Registry was learning by its errors and at the expense of its clients. Decisions as to the registrability of a trade mark rested with the Registrar or his Assistant. There was the possibility of appeal to the Commissioners, two of whom were the Law Officers. Opponents of registration[23] felt that relatively junior civil servants were now taking decisions formerly left to the courts. The journal *Engineering* commented that classification "would do very well for the arrangement of goods at an exhibition" predicting that it would prove utterly useless. In one respect they were right; in the hasty preparations of December 1875, the only classification to hand was that used for the 1851 Exhibition. The new Registry with its improvised crew got under way to a chorus of criticism, but kept afloat and made progress.

Woodcroft retires[24]

In January 1876 W.H. Smith II at the Treasury wrote to the Lord Chancellor: "My Lords have been given to understand that Mr Woodcroft contemplated retirement and they are prepared to receive an application for awarding him a pension". Thus Victorian governments put the retiring servant in the position of suppliant, though except in the case of serious misdemeanours such as those of Edmunds, pensions were routinely granted. In March following, the Patent Commissioners, in the person of their secretary H.J.L. Graham, wrote to the Treasury[25] that, since Mr Woodcroft's retirement, now a fact, they had been endeavouring to find a successor to fill the offices of Clerk to the Commissioners, Superintendent of the Patent Museum, and Registrar of Trade Marks and Designs. They had been unable to find anyone so suited by age and attainments as Mr H. Reader Lack, "who has shown himself most efficient in the somewhat difficult duties" (of Registrar of Trade Marks) "as he had previously done in the office which he holds at the Board of Trade".

They had offered him the appointment, but:

> that gentleman does not think that the difference between his present emoluments and the salary proposed for the new office is sufficient to warrant him relinquishing his post at the Board of Trade for the more laborious office....He intimates, however, to the Commissioners his willingness to place his services and experience of 28 years of official life at their disposal if the salary of the new

office were to be fixed at £1,500 at the commencement instead of after 5 years of service.

The Commissioners of Patents recommended acceptance; pomposity can seldom have achieved such a victory over the Treasury. Lack's was a very large salary by the standards of the ordinary Civil Service, indeed as Lingen at the Treasury pointed out[26] in a long letter to the Commissioners, the highest, with very few exceptions. It was not to be a precedent; Lack was initially seconded from the Board of Trade for this exacting post.

Lack had been able to write[27] privately to Lingen for advice, which was to accept, as the post was likely to become an important one in an expanding office. There is a suggestion of collusion in the situation.

Did Woodcroft resign gladly or was he to some extent pushed? As he was the hero of the early years at the office and might have merited exceptional consideration, the question inevitably poses itself. Certainly he had ample reason to call it a day; he was in his 73rd year and had complained several times of infirmity. Since the 1860s he had complained of lumbago and chest problems: a month before his retirement at the end of March 1876 he had written to Stuart Wortley at the Patent Museum (see below Ch. 13) that he was away, suffering from bronchitis and gout. The handwriting of all his late letters is shaky and sometimes barely legible.

Both Lack and Stuart Wortley were much younger and evidently ambitious men. The journal *Engineering*, ever watchful of Patent Office affairs, cautiously welcomed Lack's arrival[28] and while regretting he was not a technical man, recognised that he was "a good solid man of business". Woodcroft was a "person of strikingly original and liberal views and inventors owe him much" but the journal suggested that he was no administrator and in recent years had been carried by the excellent clerks. Woodcroft undoubtedly resented[29] Stuart Wortley's assertiveness at the Museum and included him with Edmunds, Henry Cole and Atkinson (surely most unfairly) among those he preferred "as enemies rather than as friends".

If any time seems to mark the beginning of the end of the loosely controlled office that Woodcroft had known, it was this year, 1876. The

91

Treasury was tightening its grip on management as the Office rapidly grew bigger and more bureaucratic.

One of Woodcroft's last official duties was to advise the Commissioners on which competitive examinations and subjects were best for recruiting new staff – an ironic role for the man who started life "at the loom" and who had no formal academic qualifications. In January this year he had to answer a formidable questionnaire from Lingen concerning amongst other things the Office's legal accountability for the information in its publications, "replies in the half-margin".

This was part of an enquiry ordered by the Chancellor the previous December, and carried out by Lingen and the Master of the Rolls, Sir George Jessel. When submitting the report, W.H. Smith at the Treasury touched on its findings: "My Lords approve generally of the principles, namely the concentration of all the functions of the Patent Office under a single permanent officer, with assistants and deputy assistants at the head of its several branches". This, an obvious outcome of the Edmunds affair in part, anticipates the organisation under the 1883 Act (Ch.11). There was criticism in the Commons of the government's refusal to publish the report, especially as it touched on the future of the Patent Museum (see Ch.13).

There was thus no shortage of possible reasons for Woodcroft's departure. His leaving surely merited mention in the Commissioners' *Annual Report* for 1876, but there was none; he was the first head of the modern Patent Office (omitting Edmunds) and the only one not to be honoured in some way. He was granted a fairly generous pension of £800 (perhaps £40,000 now). He had been elected a Fellow of the Royal Society in 1859; his sponsors included I.K. Brunel and Sir Francis Palgrave.

For various reasons he was unable to make a clean break with the Office. His principal link was the younger Richard Prosser, who may not have improved his standing with the authorities as a result. Woodcroft's letters during the last three years of his life are much taken up with his efforts, using his official papers, to establish ownership of models, and portraits at South Kensington, and the value of books still owned by him (and perhaps other institutions) in the Patent Office Library. They are also much taken up with ill-health, and his undying interest in the history of technology.

30 Redcliffe Gardens
South Kensington, SW.
3rd January, 1877

Dear Richard,

I have not been able to get to the Office as I proposed, Gout and Lumbago keep me an unwilling prisoner. But I think something is also due to the present wretched weather. If you will kindly take charge of the notes from Mr White of the Royal Society and the Librarian of the Literary and Philosophical Society of Manch.r respecting the books that have been sent to me by each society I shall be much obliged. And also Mr Atkinson's list of my books in the Library other than those I have named.

Yours truly,

B. Woodcroft

Woodcroft's concern with ownership of items which had been in public collections for so long may seem petty and unworthy of him but he may have been considering his wife's circumstances; she was to outlive him by 24 years (See Ch.13).

He died on the 7th of February, 1879 at his home in South Kensington, and was buried in Brompton Cemetery. The press made up for the Commissioners' neglect of his memory, with generous notices[30], predictably in the technical journals and provincial newspapers, but also in scientific journals such as *Nature* and *Scientific American*.

Between Woodcroft's retirement at the end of March 1876 and the fundamental "Chamberlain" Act of 1883 there were other important changes and continued expansion. Reader Lack, the new Clerk of the Commissioners, inherited Marwick Michell as his private secretary, a post of some potential.

There were continuing and weightier complaints of the inadequacy of the early (and enthusiastically received) search aids, the indexes and abridgments. In 1878 these resulted in the appointment of a Special Indexing Group[31]. Doubts had been expressed earlier in the century as to where suitable people might be found; the situation now was very different, there was an increasing supply of young men with scientific or technical training. The first six of what was to become the new profession of patent examiner[32] were appointed in August 1878. They were J. Gray, J.M.H. Munro, H. Hatfield, A. Cliff, A.J. Walke and W. Martin. They had sat papers in Précis, Geometry, Mechanical Drawing, Mechanics and Mechanism, and Hydrostatics. Only two were graduates, Munro with a D.Sc. and Gray with a B.Sc. (Edin.) and some people may be disappointed that they got the top marks in the competitive exam. A further seven would be appointed in 1881. Woodcroft's former protégé R. B. Prosser was moved from what was probably an uncongenial post in Trade Marks to head the new group, a move that proved even less congenial. His second in command was a clerk from the Specification Division, F.W. Tabrum.

In April, 1880 there was a substantial reorganisation[33] of the Office. The former rather crude "divisions" became "branches", a nomenclature that would take the Office into the 20th century. The new Patent Branch was the old Division largely unchanged apart from the loss of two First Class clerks (A.J. Prothero and T.A. Sims) both from the founding seven of 1852. The Specification Division was split up into a new Abridgment Branch with a staff of four, and a Printing and Drawing Branch with six, reflecting the current importance of publications to aid searching. The recently formed special indexers were not affected. The Commissioners' domain under Lack as Clerk now comprised the Patent, Printing, Indexing, Special Indexing, Abridgments and Sales Branches, the Library, Museum and the two Registries with a total staff of 79.

At the same time, William Marwick Michell, already private secretary[34] to Lack and second in the hierarchy, was made a Principal. A year later on the sudden disappearance on leave of the Chancellor's nephew Capt.Cairns, Michell became also Assistant Registrar of Designs and Trade Marks. In November 1882 he was also made Superintendent of the whole indexing and abridging staff but lost the private secretaryship. His Principal's salary of £500 was raised to £800, an extraordinary increase when the usual annual increment was £25. This was however Michell's zenith as, in 1883, Lowry Whittle returned[35] from his enforced transfer to the Lunacy office, reassumed his posts as Assistant Registrar of the Designs and Trade Mark Registries and became Assistant Clerk of the Commissioners. He was thus placed to be Deputy when Lack became Comptroller in 1884, but was disappointed as J. Clark Hall was appointed from the Board of Trade. William Marwick Michell had aspired[36] to the post, according to his obituary in *The Engineer*.

Notes to Chapter 10

1	As they reported	Commissioners' Report, 1875, p.10.
2	Copyright of designs	Davenport, N. *United Kingdom Copyright and Design Protection, a Brief History.* Emsworth 1993. Bell, Quentin, *The Schools of Design*, Routledge, 1963.
3	The Registry .. was on a modest scale	Harding, H. Ms Notebook gives the names. BLSRIS SC. Names of staff in this and later chapters are based on Patent Office Staff Register; and Lists *Royal Kalendars; Whittakers Almanac.*
4	Quality Court	*Post Office Directory*, 1875, 1876.
5	The Trade Marks Registry opened here	*A Century of Trade Marks*, HMSO, 1976, p.20.
6	Whittle was an MA and barrister	Board of Trade Committee on the Patent Office. (Herschell Committee) 1888. Report, Trade Marks, Minutes, Whittle, Q.1723.
7	a minor dynasty of Lack	Harrison, J. *The Judgment of Lack and the Treaty of Paris*, POESM
8	Anglo-French Trade Treaty	Harrison, as cited. Lack papers, PRO BT 191-7.
9	a slim explanatory volume	H.R. Lack, ed, *The French Treaty and Tariff of 1860, with a historical sketch*....Cassell, 1861.
10	He represented it in Vienna	Harrison, as cited.
11	Comptroller of Corn Returns	Harrison, as cited.
12	Trade marks are an elusive	Patent Office, *A Century of Trade marks*, pp.4-7.
13	until the 1875 Act	Ibid, p.4.
14	an attempt to legislate	Select Committee on the Trade Marks Bill, Report, 6.5.1862.
15	stress and evident confusion	*A Century of Trade Marks*, pp.20,22.
16	aroused widespread opposition	E.g. *Engineering*, 21, 17.3.1876; 23.6.1876.

17 especially in the textile industries — *A Century of Trade Marks*, pp.32-36; *Engineering*, 21, 31.3.1876.

18 a Manchester branch. — Commissioners Report, 1876, p.8; *A Century of Trade Marks*, pp.32-36.

19 Needle manufacturer — Commissioners' Report, 1878, p.10.

20 Sheffield Cutlers — *A Century of Trade Marks*, p.36.

21 the Chancellor, Lord Cairns, retired Mr Wylde — Harrison, *Mr Jackson and his Poetic friend* pt I, POESM 220, 10.1982; *Whittakers Almanac* 1880s.

22 William Marwick Michell — Staff Registers, vol.I.

23 Opponents of registration — *Engineering*, 21, 31.3.1876, p.261.

24 Woodcroft retires — Treasury to Chancellor, 20.1.1876. Ledger, *Correspondence with the Treasury*, III. BLSRIS SC

25 Graham wrote to the Treasury — Ibid, Letter, 24.3.1876. *Correspondence with the Treasury*, as cited.

26 as the Treasury pointed out — Lingen to Chancellor, 27.3.1876 (copy). Correspondence with the Treasury. 3, as cited.

27 Lack had been able to write — Harrison, J. *The Judgment of Lack*, POESM. (from PRO BT 191-7.)

28 welcomed Lack's arrival — *Engineering*, 21, 7.4.1876, p.283.

29 Woodcroft undoubtedly resented — Letter to R.B.Prosser, 3.2.1877, BLSRIS SC, Memorial Book.

30 Woodcroft, generous notices — *Scientific American*, 22.3.1879; *The Engineer*, 14.2.1879; *Manchester Guardian*, 11.2.1879; *Sheffield Independent*, 13.2.1879; *Iron*, 15.2. 1879.

31 Special Indexing Group — Patent Office, Staff; Annual Return, 1878; Harding p.30.

32 patent examiner — Establishment List, 1893. Harding, H. *Notes on the History of the Examining Staff*. t.script of talk, 1926, BLSRIS.

33 substantial reorganisation — Staff Return, 1880.

34 Michell, already private secretary — Staff Register, Michell.

35 Lowry Whittle returned — Harrison, J. *M.J. Jackson... POESM 220.10.1982*. Patent Office Enquiry (Herschell) 1887. Whittle evidence, 7.5.1887, Q.1223.

36 William Marwick Michell had aspired — Obituary, *The Engineer*, 27.3.1885, p.288.

11 The end of the Commissioners – "Chamberlain's Act", 1883

This period of change and expansion in the Office was nevertheless one of no change in patent law, despite the many shortcomings revealed by the 1872 Committee and its recommendations. This was not from lack of debate of the most pressing issues of patent law reform. Between 1875 and 1883 a series of bills[1] were drafted and abandoned. This lack of progress was less the result of continued antagonism to patents than of the inherent problems. Among the short-lived bills were those of Lord Chancellor Cairns (1875) and the Attorney General, John Holker in 1877. During 1881/2 a bill drawn up by members of the Glasgow Philosophical Society[2] and introduced by George Anderson, an industrialist and MP for the City, achieved a second reading; it was backed by Lord Kelvin. A Society of Arts bill[3] was introduced by Sir John Lubbock. The progress – or lack of it – of the bills was accompanied by lively debate in the technical press and among professional bodies.

Consciousness of the artisan inventor had been articulated many years before by Dickens. It was now accepted that the £25 initial cost of a patent was prohibitive for the working man, and the 1852 procedure still too complicated. (In 1877 the Crown Office was questioning the continued use of the Great Seal for routine documents.) The system of 3 and 7-year payments had proved its value but there was disagreement as to the periods and the amounts. Should a patent last longer than 14 years, and what should be the procedure for extending it?– the traditional Privy Council system was expensive and unpopular. The question of official examination occupied most debate. A proposal that additional unpaid commissioners should act as examiners was rejected. Even the difficult question of examination for novelty was considered. There was a beginning acceptance that professional examination of some kind[4] was essential but that a government official should be empowered to deny an Englishman a patent was still too novel for many. (That he might actually assist the patentee was not considered.) There was some suspicion of government appointees: a letter to the journal *Engineering* from an applicant who had sat the general civil service exam, stressing its academic and unpractical character, provoked the editorial comment that government clerks were "absolutely ignorant of the subject to be dealt with"[5]. This was linked to this journal's sniping at the new head of the Office. Just at this time the first staff to join under the Playfair scheme "to attract men of liberal education" had been appointed (among them A.E. Housman). These were the new "ten till four young gentlemen"[6] referred to by the same journal.

The 16th of April, 1883, was an important day for patent law and for the Office; it was the occasion of Joseph Chamberlain's[7] moving a second reading of a new government bill[8] (known as no 3) which became the basis of the Patents, Designs and Trade Marks Act the same year. Chamberlain had been appointed President of the Board of Trade in 1880 on the formation of Gladstone's second government. He was the first outstanding politician with a first-hand grasp of the principles of patents. The fortunes of his family firm[9] of Nettlefold and Chamberlain had been founded on the purchase of rights in American screw-making machinery shown at the 1851 Exhibition.

Interrupted only once (by Parnell) he gave a masterly account and justification of the principles adopted. Arguments in favour of patent law were now superfluous. "In recent years there had been a very great change of opinion". He summarised the fourfold objects of a good patent law:

- the protection granted should be adequate without creating an undue monopoly

- the cost should not be so great as to put them out of reach of any class

- protection should be as real and effectual as possible

- litigation where unavoidable should be both cheap and efficient, (the last a fine example of 19th century optimism).

He had taken a personal interest in the detail drafting, consulting with officials[10] such as Lack. He dealt at length with the question of examination, rejecting examination for novelty as impractical, and echoing some of the technical press when he feared that examiners "might stifle the inventive genius of the country". "Inventors would never accept any system which left them absolutely at the mercy of a select class of officials". Patent litigation had revealed the expertise and high cost involved in settling such issues. The examination under the bill would be confined to seeing that the invention was a proper subject for a patent and that the provisional and complete specifications agreed. (One examiner in this century[11] has called this coming to the right decision for the wrong reasons.) It was right for the time, but not for all time.

The Bill included a measure for compulsory licensing on reasonable terms. Chamberlain reminded the House that "it would have been possible for the German inventor of the hot-blast furnace [Bessemer] if he had chosen to refuse a licence in England to have destroyed almost the whole iron industry in this country". He claimed that this had happened in the case of coal tar dyes.

Under the bill, provisional protection would be provided for a mere £1, and the grant for a further £3. The first subsequent payment would be after 4 years instead of 3, so an artisan could get a 4-year patent for £4. Chamberlain's frank estimates of the loss to the Exchequer was the first official admission of the value of patent revenue. The first year of a new law might reduce it from £160,000 to £2,000, with £60,000 spent on improving indexes and abridgments. The expected large increase in applications would not at first compensate.

Some members had opposed the subsequent payments of £50 and £100. Chamberlain hoped they would not ask more of the Treasury: "the change proposed was so great, and the benefits so large... the working classes would declare that what was offered should be taken without delay".

The bill provided for the replacement of the Patent Commissioners by a single comptroller. George Anderson, the Glasgow member, questioned the change. Chamberlain's reply[12] was sufficient explanation for their demise: "he had never defended the management of the Office by the law officers, because the law officers had never managed it". This was a little unfair to Romilly and others who had at least tried.

After some amendments by the Standing Committee[13] on Trade, the Act became law on the 25th of August, 1883. It was a high point of

Chamberlain's career. "It has been a triumphant session for you" wrote John Morley.[14] J.L. Garvin's more recent comment[15] that "the Patent Office was now adequately staffed and its whole organisation improved" was not so apt.

The Act was to come into force on the 1st of January, 1884. It was radical both as regards patent law and the administration of the Office. In addition to reduced fees and a simpler procedure for the patentee, "scientifically trained examiners were introduced to determine whether an invention was properly the subject matter of a patent, whether its nature and the way in which it was to be carried into effect were clearly described and whether the complete specification agreed with the provisional and comprised one invention only. The documents were to be thrown open to inspection for a period prior to sealing…in order that persons interested could oppose the grant; powers to amend specifications were given and arrangements made for improving the indexes and providing illustrated abridgments. The Board of Trade was given power to grant compulsory licences"[16].

The Commissioners ceased to exist, authority passed to a single Comptroller acting under the Board of Trade. Harding has aptly stressed[17] how, in clause after clause of the Act the phrases "the Comptroller shall" or "the Comptroller may" occur, whether relating to judicial, managerial or merely formal matters such as sealing with the Office seal as proxy for the Great Seal.

"The multifarious duties to be performed by the Comptroller were, of course, actually to be performed by subordinates". The Office was late in adopting the system of delegated responsibilities in other parts of the government service; even recent thinking on its reform had not gone beyond the notion of creating more Commissioners to act as examiners and retaining the function of the Law Officers. Their role would now be to hear appeals from the decisions of the Comptroller or his deputy, with the courts as a last resort. One of the Commissioners' – or Woodcroft's – successes, the Patent Museum, was transferred to the Machinery Department of the South Kensington Museum. The Act reaffirmed the royal prerogative: the Crown could withhold, annul or, where the safety of the realm was concerned, take over a patent on its own terms. (This in relation to instruments and munitions of war had existed since 1859.)

As sitting head of the Office, Reader Lack became the first Comptroller. It had been an eventful year for him: in March 1883 the Board of Trade had reluctantly released him[18] at the demand of the Foreign Office to represent Britain at the signing of the Paris Convention[19] for the Protection of Industrial Property. Eleven strangely diverse nations (e.g. France and Salvador, Belgium and Guatemala) had contracted that subjects of other nations in the union should enjoy the same rights as their own as regards patents, trade marks and designs. At this stage Britain was not a signatory, as the 1883 Act was not in force. Lack had also attended the preliminary diplomatic meeting in 1880.

Hitherto patent protection had been entirely national in scope; the holder of a significant invention had to take out individual patents in the various countries and was subject to their patent laws. Before 1852 an English patent for a foreign patented invention could remain in force after the expiry of the foreign one or could even be obtained by "communicating from abroad" an invention unpatented elsewhere. Harmonising or "assimilating", in Victorian-speak, patent law internationally had been on the agenda of reformers for many years. The 1871-2 Patent Law enquiry reported that there should be an assimilation in the law and practice amongst the various civilised countries and that Her Majesty's government be requested to enquire of foreign and colonial governments how far they are ready to concur. While the 1883 Act was in gestation in the 1870s, British delegates took part in several international meetings; C.W. Siemens was President and Thomas Webster Vice-President of the Vienna Patent Congress in August 1873. A paper on assimilation by a British patent agent, William Lloyd Wise read to an international law reform meeting at The Hague in 1875 led to the formation of a committee of lawyers to consider it.

Britain signed the Convention in March, 1884, and ratified it on June 6. Its provision of most immediate importance concerned priority: an applicant in a member country would not lose priority through the delay in applying in another, priority could be back dated within a certain period of grace. Membership of the Convention grew slowly: the United States did not join until 1887, and Germany until 1903. The Paris Convention was the progenitor of the Berne Copyright Convention (1887) and the present international bureaux and secretariats concerned with the protection of all forms of intellectual property.

In the autumn of 1883 the Board of Trade and the Treasury had to consider the important matter of staffing, in view of the anticipated avalanche of applications in January. A Mr John Clark Hall was transferred[20] from the Finance department of the Board to be Deputy Comptroller from the New Year, on the grounds of his experience with a large staff. He had no legal or technical experience, a portent of trouble in a job that needed both. At the end of November the first advertisements for Assistant Examiners appeared[21]. (As yet there were no Examiners, strictly speaking.) As was now usual, entry would be by competitive examination. The age limits were stringent, 21–25. Starting salary was £250 rising to £400. The journal *Engineering* was scathing[22]: what was wanted was men of wide practical experience, not young graduates, however well qualified. The new men had not arrived when the new regime commenced.

The Office of the Commissioners of Patents for Inventions had exemplified a very British gradualism, an incomplete break with outmoded tradition and failure to establish new methods for new problems. On the other hand the Commissioners had at least lent their authority to some real achievements in official publishing and to the establishment of a new museum and national library.

Notes to Chapter 11

1 a series of bills — Harding, *Patent Office Centenary*, pp.24,125.

2 Glasgow Philosophical Society — *Engineering*, 29, June 1880, p.504.

3 Society of Arts bill — Ibid, *32*, 5.8.1881.

4 examination of some kind — Ibid, *31*, 1881, p.617.

5 Government clerks were absolutely ignorant — Ibid, *24*, 20.7.1877, p.51.

6 "ten till four young gentlemen" — Ibid, *36*, 31.8. 1883, p.199.

7 the occasion of Joseph Chamberlain — *Hansard* 16.4.1883, pp.350-394. Garvin, J.L. *The Life of Joseph Chamberlain*, Macmillan, 1952-69, Vol.1, pp.419-420.

8 a new Government bill — *Engineering*, 35, 23.3.1883, p.275.

9 The fortunes of his family firm — Garvin, p.419.

10 consulting with officials Notes on the Patent Bill, MS, signed "JC", in PRO, BT209-443.

11 one examiner in this century Harding, H. *Notes on the History of the Examining Staff*, t.s. of talk, 1926, BLSRIS SC.

12 Chamberlain's reply Hansard, as cited, p.363.

13 amendments by the Standing Committee Report, 9.7.1883.

14 John Morley Garvin, cited, p.420.

15 Garvin's more recent comment *Life*, as cited.

16 scientifically trained examiners Harding, *Centenary*, p.28.

17 Harding has aptly stressed Ibid, p.37.

18 had reluctantly released him Harrison, J. *The Judgment of Lack...POESM.*

19 the Paris Convention Bosch, Arpad, *The Paris Convention*, 1883-1893. International Convention for the Protection of Industrial Property, Geneva, 1983. Introduction & pp. 117,266.

Davis, I.J.G. and Harrison, J. *Prelude to the UK's accession to the Paris Convention, March 17,1884,* J. Ind. Prop. Nov, 1984, pp.395-399.

20 J. Clark Hall was transferred Board of Trade Enquiry into the Patent Office, (Herschell). Report, 1877. J.C. Hall's evidence 10.4.1886, Q. 836,839-841.

21 advertisements for Assistant Examiners *Engineering* 36, 30.11.1853, p.308.

22 *Engineering* was scathing 37, 1884, p.189.

12 Postscript: the first patent examiners

On January 4, 1884, the journal *The Engineer* reported[1]:

> Unusual activity prevailed at the Patent Office on the lst Inst., when the new Patent Act came into operation. One enthusiastic inventor hailing from north of the Tweed took up his station outside the door soon after midnight, and his patience was rewarded by the honour of appearing as "No 1" under the new law. Towards 4 o'clock he was joined by two others and when the hour of opening had arrived a small crowd of about fifty eager applicants had assembled but when they had been disposed of business became slack. There was however a steady influx, and at 4 o'clock it was found that 266 applications had been recorded. This is by far the largest ever received in one day.

One former member of staff (M.J. Jackson, see below) wrote[2] that the office was "literally besieged".

The first of the new assistant examiners was not in place until mid-January and the existing special indexing staff, Hatfield and his co-entrants plus the intake of 1881 (as described in Ch.10) bore the brunt.

There were as many applications[3] for patents in the first quarter of 1884 as in the whole of the previous year and this resulted in another period of urgent recruitment. Six more assistant examiners[4] were appointed in January 1884 and another eighteen later in the year. Eight were appointed in 1885 and again in 1886. The vacancies were greatly oversubscribed[5]: 200 competed for 42 vacancies in 1884-5. (The successful prided themselves that even the unsuccessful became professors or went on to otherwise distinguished careers.) When the first of the new staff had arrived in 1884 two of the original indexing group (Walke and Cliff) were made Examiners[6] to superintend the work of the Assistants, an arrangement that went down badly with some of them. Prosser was made Superintending Examiner[7] though not for long.

The examining staff have been described as the first scientific civil servants.

Even Harding, the partisan and charitable chronicler of the Office and a former examiner conceded[8] that "the first years after the passing of the 1883 Act were times of great difficulty". The Office had new tasks and many new staff; the patent system itself was still in a state of transition. There were internal stresses and a positive barrage of external criticism, some of it cogent but more misguided. Those who had opposed the introduction of examining found plenty which seemed to vindicate them

Among the difficulties, the greatest was that of "interferences"[9]. A last-minute clause in the Act (7, (5)) required that when two concurrent applications appeared to be for the same invention, the examiner should notify the Comptroller who could refuse the second, subject to appeal to the Law Officer. The clause was well intended; it was unfair that an applicant should spend time and fees on a patent that would be immediately invalid, and pernicious that two patents should be granted for the same invention. (If not intercepted in the office, appeal against the grant could be lodged after acceptance of the complete specification.) With applications at some 17,000 a year the problem of scrutinising and identifying interfering specifications can be imagined; Lack told the Herschell Committee in 1886 that interferences required time equivalent to the work of ten assistant examiners. There was ample scope for the later applicant to feel unfairly treated. There were calls for the return of examination[10] to the Law Officers. Generally the press was not sympathetic to the problems of administering the Act: the Office was accused of not recruiting more examiners in time and of having to transfer much needed indexers[11]; new rules for supplying small drawings for the illustrated abridgments were pettifogging[12] – "Dickens' well known strictures on the Barnacle family are aptly illustrated". Minor flaws in drafting were pointed out; an innovation of the Act enabled a provincial applicant to apply on a special form available at post offices but if he dated it earlier than January 1, 1884 it would be refused, thus an English inventor might be denied parity with a foreigner whose agent could apply in person.

In referring to press criticism[13] of the Office, Harding was a little economical with the truth in not adding that the best informed and thus most telling came from a former assistant examiner. M.J. Jackson had joined the special indexing staff in 1882 as one of the intake of young science graduates who later formed the first assistant examiners in 1884.

105

In 1887 he resigned to take a teaching post in India. His criticisms were in two unusually long letters[14] in December 1887 and January 1888 to the journal *Engineering*, never behindhand in attacking the Office. In the first letter Jackson presented a picture of an Office where the indexers had been thrown into the new work of examining with no preparation and inadequate instructions and where the supervising examiner (Prosser) had not yet been appointed. Despite this the young technical staff coped adequately – to the extent that the Comptroller commended their work in a report to the Treasury – until red tape was imposed via the two examiners Walke and Cliff who tinkered with and mutilated their reports. The assistant examiners had specialised in certain subjects, experience which was now wasted and their morale destroyed. In May 1884 eleven of them complained to the President of the Board of Trade in a long memorial which was ignored.

Before expanding on how the work of examination was failing patentees, the second letter attacked the competence of the senior management; the working of the new law required:

> that the heads of the Office should combine with high administrative powers the greatest scientific and technical as well as legal knowledge. It is unfortunate that the Board of Trade should have thought to appoint to the two most important posts in the Office gentlemen who cannot fairly lay claim to any of these. Not only is this important from a public point of view but it is unsatisfactory from an official point of view, as it is extremely demoralising to the men in the Office to feel sure, as they do, that neither the Comptroller nor Deputy can properly appreciate their work.

Jackson castigated the management in the manner of a senior prefect reporting on the tone of his school to the governors: "it would be difficult for me adequately to describe what may be called the tone of the Office, which is thoroughly unsatisfactory". He described "this unhappy Office" where sycophancy ("toadying") flourished and individuality earned a bad name. In appeals and decision-making, the Comptroller and Deputy Comptroller's weakness and vacillation had prevented the development of a consistent "practice of the Office". Examiners had been first ordered not to report interferences until complete specifications were received: "When the complaints became too loud and too numerous to ignore, we were ordered to return to the original practice". He charged the Office with failing the intentions of the Act as regards interferences and the rules that the provisional and complete specifications should agree and be for one invention only. After a list of improper practices such as false dating of records, he commented, "as to the work of examination itself, it has drifted under the present management from bad to worse until it has now become in all its essential features, a dead letter".

Was he fair to a management struggling to administer new and revolutionary measures? One examiner recalled[15] in the 1920s, "he (Lack) has been in my opinion, unfairly abused. He had no special technical knowledge any more than some Law Officers, but he was a man of ability somewhat curtailed by a slow and cautious manner". The same examiner remembered "going out for lunch one day (in 1895) and finding promenading before the door a sandwichman with boards reading 'Lack of Judgment' ". Harding's history is silent concerning the episode.

Confirmation of the difficulties came in the appointment of another enquiry soon after the Act. The Herschell Committee[16] appointed by the Board of Trade in 1886 to enquire into "the duties, organisation and arrangements" of the Office, with regard to examination and to trade marks and designs, heard evidence on the former in 1886 and on the latter during 1887 (before its first session Sir T. Farrer Herschell became Lord Chancellor). The Committee included the veteran of patent enquiries Sir Bernhard Samuelson and Sir Richard Webster (1842–1915) son of Thomas Webster the reformer and a future Lord Chief Justice.

Predictably, no direct reference to the state of affairs criticised by Jackson was made in the two published reports. On patent examination the main recommendations were the dropping of the notification to the applicants of interferences, and the rigour of the "one invention only" rule, both in the direction of laxity. In recommending some reduced supervision of the assistant examiners but only when experienced (thus providing more indexers) the report partly conceded Jackson's point. Increased staff were recommended for Trade Marks and – yet again – the provision of an adequate building.

In his letters Jackson called for another enquiry, which would be "ashamed to follow Lord Herschell's example, who had the

107

extraordinary temerity to present to Parliament a partial report, without the least indication that it merely contained a selection of the evidence". References to individual staff would have been improper perhaps, but such scruples did not apply in the case of Edmunds in 1865.

Official decisions often look perverse, and there is apparent perversity in the premature retirement of the Superintending Examiner, R.B. Prosser and his assistant, F.W. Tabrum, in April 1888 following the Herschell enquiry. They were the only officials singled out for praise by Jackson[17], Prosser in particular for "his unvarying courtesy and abilities", and his "wider knowledge of patents than all the rest of this department put together, yet he seems to be the object of special aversion to the Board of Trade". Jackson's praise is impressive, coming from one of the "young turks" of the new technical staff, whereas Prosser was an old hand from the Woodcroft era. These retirements were not a spiteful response to Jackson's letters, but had been hanging over the two from much earlier. "This happened", Jackson wrote, "in 1885, and the Board of Trade determined to cause him to retire but the project was foiled by the energy of the then President, Mr Stanhope".

Prosser's examination[18] by the Committee was oddly brief and perfunctory; none of the problems besetting the examining staff was raised, they seemed mainly interested in getting admission that he had not enough to do.

Such speculation about his retirement is prompted by his special place in the history of the Office and Library (see Ch.7).

Suppression of the sensitive part of "Herschell" and the retirements provoked[19] more protesting leaders in the senior engineering journals. A Parliamentary question[20] and call for disclosure received the official reply that it would "not be in the interests of the service". The journal *Engineering* attributed the removal of Mr Clark Hall[21], the Deputy Comptroller, to a non-Patent Office job, and of Mr Whittle, the Deputy Registrar of Trade Marks, to the secret report (Jackson had directly attacked the competence of Clark Hall). "When was there not something wrong with the Patent Office", sighed the writer in *The Engineer*. Correspondents' complaints of the cost in pensions of early retirements had a curiously modern ring.

According to examining staff tradition, set down by Harding[22] in the 1920s (he is silent about Jackson), Prosser was not suited to the new problems and pressures of the time. When the special indexing staff were recruited his system was said to be unsatisfactory and much of the work had to be done again later. Perhaps his antiquarian interests imply the wrong temperament for the time. "He had been promised a 'position of ease and dignity' ". Harding comments, "it was anything but that". Prosser's retiring "compensation allowance" of £520 confirms that his was indeed an early retirement.

Moses Jackson is of course mainly known not as the critic of Patent Office management but as the friend of the Office's most interesting and unlikely employee, A.E. Housman, who worked in the Trade Marks Registry from late 1882 until his extraordinary translation to the chair of Latin at University College, London, in May 1892.

Housman was the eldest child of a well connected but unstable and improvident solicitor practising near Bromsgrove, Worcestershire. After winning prizes in Latin and Greek at Bromsgrove School, in 1877 he won a valuable scholarship to Trinity College, Oxford, to read for an honours degree in Classics ("Greats"). He shared a college staircase with A.W. Pollard, the future Keeper of Printed Books at the British Museum and bibliographer, and began his lifelong and largely unrequited homosexual affection for Jackson. The son of the owner of a private school in Ramsgate, Jackson was reading science... "Jackson was an athlete who rowed for his college and seems to have had a hearty contempt for literature... Given Housman's bookish tastes, his highly specialised interests, his lack of enthusiasm for games, the basis of friendship was not an obvious one"[23]. When they moved out of College the three took rooms together.

Housman did well in the first public examination ("Mods") but in May 1881 famously and – in view of his expectations – disastrously failed his Finals. The other two both got Firsts. His unscheduled classical studies, his contempt for Oxford's classics teaching and the distractions of Jackson do not fully account for the failure. There was bad news from home, where his father was ill and their finances precarious. Housman returned to Bromsgrove, did some supply teaching, and returned to Oxford for a term to read for a pass degree, his scholarship cancelled.

He obtained his pass degree in 1882 and was successful in the competitive Civil Service exam in London. He joined the Service under the Playfair scheme designed to encourage men with a liberal education who would otherwise go into the professions to become the misleadingly called "Higher Division Clerks" – their rank was lower than the Upper Division. The following November he began work in the Trade Marks Registry.

Joining the government service was a natural step for one in Housman's situation but it is not known how he managed to enter the same office as Jackson, who was already working[24] in the Indexing branch – not yet an assistant examiner as stated by Page. It is agreed it could hardly have been a coincidence but may not have been difficult as the small staff in Trade Marks was increasing. The head of the Registry[25] was J.L. Whittle, the Deputy Registrar and not R.Griffin (*pace* Page) who came later. Housman's work was checking new applications for trademarks against the registers and for conformity with the law; though it made him a satrap of a banal commercial world and has been generally thought to be tedious, it did need discrimination and a sense of the law. One biographer, Page, has described it as resembling "a bizarre travesty of the process of editing a classical text"[26]. A few files initialled AEH are said to survive in the present Registry. The salary was miserable[27], £100, rising by small increments; the year before he left it was only £171. Pay for such Higher Division clerks was greatly inferior to that of comparable young technical staff. The Victorian Treasury, progressives might think, had its priorities right.

After lodging by himself for a while Housman moved in with Jackson and his younger brother Adalbert at 82 Talbot Rd, also in Bayswater. According to Housman's brother Laurence, recalling it later in life, Housman's friendship with Adalbert[28] was fond and more openly physical than his more circumspect relationship with Moses, certainly it was very close. After Jackson's emigration it was a means of keeping in touch.

In late 1885 occurred the much speculated upon schism and "fugue"; some kind of break with Jackson which caused Housman to disappear for several days during which Jackson was worried enough to contact Housman senior in Bromsgrove. After his reappearance Housman went into separate lodgings in Northumberland Road, Bayswater. (It has been noted that the break coincided with the introduction of harsher

110

legislation against homosexual behaviour, the "Labouchere Amendment".)

During and since Oxford he had been working on contributions to journals of classical studies; the first was published in the *Journal of Philology* in 1882. After the break with Jackson it is assumed he intensified his after-hours work in the British Museum, publishing eight papers in 1887 alone. In 1892 he applied for one of two vacant chairs, in Latin and Greek, at University College London. On the strength of his published work – now 25 papers – and some dazzling testimonials from other classical scholars he was awarded the professorship in Latin. Thus he was translated "from the gutter" as he once put it, somewhat unfairly to the Office, and began his career as a don which took him to the Kennedy chair at Cambridge.

The ten years in the Office was certainly a sombre period of unfulfilled talents for Housman, but the evidence, such as it is, does not present a picture of unrelieved gloom. Some of the warmest tributes to Housman's character came from young Patent Office colleagues. John Maycock and Ernest Kingsford had both been in the old Specification Division and moved into Abridgments and Trade Marks respectively. Maycock's recollections[29] of walking excursions in Surrey at weekends with another friend called Eyre pay tribute to the love of nature one would expect in Housman but also to a charm and humour counter to the image of the aloof acerbic professor of Latin. Maycock liked him "better than any man I ever knew", a tribute Housman kept until his death, and Griffin, his later senior in Trade Marks, wrote[30] that "no one could possibly not love him".

One of the few letters[31] from this time, referring to a Fenian bomb scare that proved a false alarm, evokes a view of Quality Court in the 1880s:

> The room I sit in is considered the likeliest place, because it has a charming deep area outside which looks as if it was made to drop a bomb into; so when this explosion was heard, several people came trooping into the room in hopes of finding corpses...

Housman gained a predictable reputation for not taking kindly to authority – an affinity with Jackson; in another letter to his step-mother from the same year, 1885, he writes:

An elaborate new index[32] of Trade Marks is being compiled... It goes on very remarkable principles which I do not quite understand. Under the head of "Biblical Subjects" is included an old monk drinking out of a tankard; and the Virgin Mary and John the Baptist are put among "Mythical Figures".

Nor was he entirely aloof from Office politics. In 1890 he drafted a letter on behalf of colleagues[33] to the Registrar of Trade Marks (Lack) complaining that P.G.L. Webb the Establishment clerk was being given Trade Marks examining to do thus giving him "a status not justified either by length of service or by acquaintance with the work..."

During his long career at the Office Webb published a volume of poems and some translations from the German.

The above incursion into developments after 1883 is perhaps justified since the debate whether to examine or not to examine patents professionally figured so largely in the preceding years.

The next major administrative change was the introduction of the investigation for novelty by an Act supplementary to that of 1883 (2 Edw. VII, c.34). It was to be limited to a 50-year search of specifications only but it entailed another large increase in staff[34]. Between 1903 and 1907, eight more examinations were held and 193 assistant examiners appointed, followed by eleven more in 1910.

To conclude, one participant describes[35] this time when job satisfaction in the examining staff was high:

> To men of my generation the ten years before the First World War were the great days of the examining staff, with about 190 assistant examiners of 20 to 30 years of age organised in 32 groups with the 60 or so staff about 20 years their senior in control. There were no women on the staff and the lower clerical duties were performed by boy clerks. Once again there was the excitement of putting into operation a new Act of Parliament and the unexplored duties of conducting the search ... No doubt experience varied but to many of us they were days of supreme enjoyment. We were not greatly troubled by salary questions, for would not the salary scale of £150 − £15 − £450 not see us safely through for the next twenty years. I

can honestly say that there was a minimum of jockeying for position with a view to future advantage, and the pleasure of working in the Office became almost entirely intellectual. Under one roof (if the Birkbeck Bank building [an annexe] may be included) were working 250 men, all scientifically trained, all experts in some branch of invention or other, and capable between them of supplying information on almost every subject under the sun.

Notes to Chapter 12

1   *The Engineer* reported   57, 1884, p.20.

2   former member of staff   *Engineering*, *44*, 30.12.1887, p.684.
    wrote

3   as many applications   *Engineering*, *38*, 1884, p.61.

4   more assistant examiners   Patent Office, *Distribution of Business & Staff*, 1893.

5   vacancies were greatly   Harding, H. *The Examining Staff 75 years on.* t.script,
    over subscribed   BLSRIS SC.

6   Walke and Cliff made   Ibid.
    Examiners

7   Prosser was made   Staff Register, vol. l, R. B. Prosser.
    Superintending Examiner

8   Even Harding…   *Notes on the History of the Examining Staff*, Pt i.
    conceded

9   "interferences"   Harding, *Centenary…* p.29.

10 calls for the return of   *The Engineer 58*, 1884, p.395.
    examination

11 transfer much needed   *Engineering*, *37*, 1884, p.11.
    indexers

12 new rules…were   Ibid, *37*, 25.1.1884, p.82.
    pettifogging

13 press criticism   Harding, *Centenary*, p.30.

14 Jackson, two long letters   *Engineering 44*, 30.12.1887, pp.684–5. *45*, 6.1.1888, p.18.

15 one examiner recalled   Wright, A.R. *Old Days in the Patent Office.* t.s. of lecture,
    21.1.1929, BLSRIS SC.

16 The Herschell
Committee

Committee Appointed by the Board of Trade to Enquire into the Duties, Organisation and Arrangements of the Patent Office under the Patents, Designs and Trade Marks Act 1883. Report (Patents) 1887,(Trade Marks and Designs) 1888.

17 praise by Jackson

Engineering, 6.1.1888, p.18.

18 Prosser's examination

Herschell, as cited, Minutes, 8.3.1886, Q.s. 485–497.

19 the retirements provoked

The Engineer, **65**, 242.1888, p.158.

20 A Parliamentary question

Engineering, **45**, 24.2.1888, p.194

21 removal of Mr Clark
Hall

Ibid, **45**, 13.1.1888, p.30.

22 set down by Harding

Notes on the History of the Examining Staff, as cited.

23 Jackson was an athlete

Page, Stephen. *A.E.H.: A Critical Biography*. Macmillan, 1983, Page, p.41.

24 Jackson, who was already
working

Harrison, J. M.J. Jackson and his Poetic Friend, POESM. 220–221, 1982–3.

25 head of the Registry

Century of Trade Marks, as cited, p.25, Page, p.49.

26 a bizarre travesty

Page, p.49.

27 salary was miserable

Patent Office, *Distribution of Business and Staff*, 1888.

28 friendship with Adalbert

Page, p.52.

29 Maycock's recollections

Ibid, p.50, 63.

30 Griffin... wrote

Letter to ? Scholfield, 19.6.1936, Trinity College, Cambridge, Add.MSS a71.

31 One of the few letters

Maas, Henry, ed. *Letters of A.E. Housman*, Hart Davis, 1971, p.27.

32 An elaborate new index

10.6. 1885, Maas, p.24.

33 letter on behalf of
colleagues

Ibid, p.27.

34 another large increase
in staff.

Harding J. *The Examining Staff, 75 Years On*. t. script.

35 one participant describes

Harding, as cited, p.3.

13 The Patent Museum (a tale of two museums)

The Patent Office Museum and Library are popularly supposed to have originated in a "suggestion of the Prince Consort" but in this fertile period for the genesis of museums and libraries matters were not quite so simple.

Prince Albert as President of the Society of Arts knew of Woodcroft's work and interests as a member. On the day the new Patent Office opened at Southampton Buildings (December 29, 1852) Woodcroft was asked to go to Windsor to explain the background to his new job. Predictably the Prince came in for a lecture on patent indexing and the evils of its lack, but also "HRH questioned Professor Woodcroft very closely as to his opinion of the probable advantage of the plan hinted at by the Exhibition Commissioners to have a place where models of new inventions might be exhibited and preserved, and where lectures might be given...exemplified by the sight at the same time of working models"[1].

Woodcroft met the Prince Consort again[2] on January 12, 1853, with Sir John Romilly the Master of the Rolls and executive Patent Commissioner (to the extent that any of them were executive at this time). These meetings are illuminating as to the mood of this post-Exhibition period and the characters of the two, the Prince with his now familiar width of interests and Woodcroft pardonably at his most enthusiastic and obsequious. They show that the Museum and Library were closely associated with the developments resulting in the acquisition of the Kensington Gore and adjacent estates and the establishment of the South Kensington Museum. The Prince was much more than a patron, and he was furthering widely held aspirations. He had already assisted in the formation of a Department of Practical Art under the Exhibition secretary, Henry Cole. A new Museum of Manufactures had opened at Marlborough House and the Central School of Design was to move from there to South Kensington.

At their first meeting Woodcroft was asked by the Prince to sound out on his behalf the reaction of industry to the museum plan. The former was about to visit the northern manufacturing towns and in late January was in touch[3] with Windsor to report progress. In Manchester he was visited by Joseph Whitworth and the consulting engineer Benjamin Fothergill who told him that the engineers and "mechanicians" of the district were about to petition the Patent Commissioners to form a library of "all known mechanical books". Woodcroft was "perplexed" at this preemption of the Prince. He consulted Sir John Romilly, who suggested delaying the memorial until a meeting of the Association of Mechanical Engineers in Birmingham.

Here on January 26, 1853, a new petition[4] was drawn up invoking the Prince Consort who,

> having suggested the great national importance (in connection with the Patent Office) of a Library and Museum containing mechanical and scientific works of every age and people for the use of the public; we the undersigned have formed ourselves into a Committee...

The names of Robert Stephenson and Joseph Whitworth led the list of great Victorian engineers. Woodcroft sent the text to the press before it had been approved in Windsor and had to conduct an embarrassing damage-limitation exercise, attempting to cancel[5] the notices and apologising. The words "in connection with the Patent Office" were at odds with the Prince's and Henry Cole's plans for South Kensington.

Woodcroft continued his mission in early February, in Manchester, Sheffield and Leeds. Meetings of civic dignitaries were held in support of the project, committees formed and petitions drawn up. His connection with petitions to the Commissioners indicates an odd detachment in his relations with them, but Romilly who had approved was one of them.

The genesis of the Museum and Library was part of a wider picture. The Exhibition Commissioners of 1851 had become a permanent body (it still exists) dedicated to the use of the large surplus fund for good causes, especially education directed to improving manufactures. Their Supplemental Charter[6] (December 1852) stated: "no measures could be so strictly in accordance with the ends of the Exhibition as those which might increase the means of industrial education and extend the influence of science and art upon productive industry".

This statement was the real origin of the Victoria and Albert Museum and indirectly of the other South Kensington institutions. The Charter was in the form of letters patent and was signed "Edmunds" as Clerk of the Patents – an irony of history in the light of his relations with Woodcroft and the museum to be.

In the early 1850's the concept of a museum and library in connection with the Patent Office became formally part of the Exhibition Commissioners' plans. Woodcroft's vision both influenced and reflected that of the great and good. The Commissioners considered possible developments under the broad classes of the Great Exhibition, thus under Machinery:

> The admirable effects produced[7] by well arranged collections of Models of Machinery, and especially of new inventions, are shown by the public importance attached to the Conservatoire des Arts et Métiers in Paris and similar institutions in other parts of Europe. The great attention paid by the public to the Department of the Exhibition devoted to Machinery indicated how eagerly such facilities for acquiring knowledge were used.

Inventors at the Patent Law enquiry (they wrote) had expressed a similar need. They set up a special committee[8] on which Woodcroft served with Lord Granville, Disraeli, Sir William Cubitt and Lyon Playfair, to consider establishing a Museum of Inventions. It recommended that it should not be confined to a mere collection of machines and models "but should embrace as complete a Library as possible of all scientific and other works related to inventions".

The museum thus became part of the plans for South Kensington. The committee also disclosed that "the Commissioners (of Patents) are taking[9] measures for the systematic collection of models" and recommended that they provide temporary accommodation for them at the Patent Office. This was the first mention in this context of what was known at the Office and had long been known to his circle, that Woodcroft already possessed a collection.

When recommending him for his post as Professor of Machinery at University College, one of his referees wrote[10], "he is extensively acquainted with the history and uses of machines". Soon after taking up the post he brought from Manchester thirty cases[11] of mechanical models on loan from the immigrant Swiss textile engineer Johann Georg Bodmer. Then in 1850, during his brief tenure at the College, he acquired from the Society of Arts many "supernumerary" models[12] from its Repository or Museum of Inventions, to serve as teaching aids. Whether or not any of these went eventually to the Patent Museum, some of the Bodmer models certainly did. (Bodmer, 1786-1864 was another engineer to die in reduced circumstances. Woodcroft helped to organise a collection[13] for his family.)

Against the date of occupation of the Southampton Buildings office (29.12.1852) Woodcroft noted moving in a "library of books and a large collection of mechanical models" to be stored "in dark corridors and rooms"[14]. Before the plans for a South Kensington Museum building were decided, Woodcroft considered adapting accommodation for them in the Patent Office: in February 1854 he wrote to E.A. Bowring[15], Registrar to the Board of Trade and an Exhibition Commissioner, complaining of the slowness of the Works department in getting vacant rooms fitted up. "I am in the hands of what is called the Board of Works, and I am sorry for it for the public's sake". The books were piled in heaps and the models – not for the last time as it proved – rusting.

In accordance with his Baconian belief that the inventor should be honoured, he had also assembled a collection of portraits of notable inventors, mainly engravings, and once more gained the Prince Consort's approval. Before any official notice of a museum of inventions, he published a notice in The Patent Journal (25th of February, 1855): "National Gallery of Portraits of Inventors, Discoverers and Introducers of Useful Arts; the following collection has been made by B. Woodcroft in the Great Seal Patent Office with a view to the formation of a National Gallery". The portraits were apparently kept in his room, perhaps for viewing on application. This first list contained some sixty inventors, from Arkwright to the Marquis of Worcester, and ended with an appeal – as with the models – for donations.

118

Once again he was well up with, if not ahead of his times. In March, 1856, Earl Stanhope (1805-1875), an enthusiast for the arts, moved the address to the Queen that was to lead to the establishment of the National Portrait Gallery. Earlier, Woodcroft had written effusively to the Earl describing his collection. The national and provincial press were reporting Patent Office developments; *The Birmingham Journal*[16] linked his name with Stanhope and *The English and American Intelligencer* suggested that here was an opportunity for international exchange – "let France say to England, 'here is our Papin, give us your Watt' ".

The development of Woodcroft's collections was thus official. In 1856 the Exhibition Commissioners reported that "Professor Woodcroft has been zealously engaged in forming the nucleus of a National Collection of Models of Inventions"[17]. Henry Cole and the Prince Consort had been considering a building to unite the various educational collections at South Kensington and had chosen a temporary iron one, a modest but possibly Crystal Palace-inspired structure. The Prince had the advice of the German architect Gottfried Semper[18] and is said to have doodled a design on blotting paper, like Paxton with his design on a railway menu. Semper's design was not used. In June 1855 the firm of Arthur Young, "Iron Buildings for Home and Abroad" sent an estimate for an "iron building suited for a museum"[19], to cost under £13,000.

When the Board of Trade approved the plans and applied to the Treasury for funds, among the still scattered collections (the Educational Museum, Museum of Manufactures and Trade Museum), destined for the new building was a "Museum of Patented Inventions now in course of formation under the Commissioners of Patents"[20]. In January 1857, before the new building was ready, Woodcroft published a full page notice in *The Patent Journal* showing the ground plan of the new building and including an invitation to apply, to those wanting to display their inventions. The name, the "Commissioners of Patents Museum" used during this early phase created an enduring but misleading image: that it was confined to patented inventions, and though many exhibits were indeed of patented inventions, the permanent contribution of the Museum to the national collections was largely because it was not confined to them.

Work went ahead with truly Victorian intensity on the utility iron building that was the first South Kensington Museum. Young's plans,

119

submitted in June 1855, were accepted in a few days. Little more than a year later Sir William Cubitt accepted[21] it on behalf of the Exhibition Commissioners. It was an iron-columned open-plan structure[22], 266 ft long and 126 ft wide, consisting of three 42 ft wide bays, with side and end galleries in the outer bays. The three cylindrical uniform roofs "like huge boilers placed side by side" as *The Builder* put it conferred the tenacious nickname the "Brompton Boilers". A generally uncomplimentary press did not understand Cole's need for a cheap building quickly. It contained 366 tons of cast and wrought iron[23], and $11\frac{1}{2}$ thousand feet of timber; a factor in its choice was that the iron could be re-used or sold – it was before the age of cheap steel.

The "Boilers" were oriented roughly north–south, and their ghost can be sensed in the present Sheepshanks gallery incorporated into the Victoria and Albert Museum; the gallery is at the north-west corner of the Boilers' site. To alleviate the iron exterior[24] the building was painted in green and white stripes. Internal decoration was by the notable John Kelk, constructor of the Albert Memorial and other London landmarks, who carried out other work at South Kensington. The old decaying buildings[25] of Brompton Park House were adapted by Cole as Museum offices, linked to the "Boilers" by a temporary brick corridor designed by James Pennethorne (who, as official architect, would design the 1867 Patent Office Library) and around which grew the first lecture and refreshment rooms of the new museum. In late 1856 and 1857 the first permanent building, the Sheepshanks Gallery, following John Sheepshanks' gift, was built in time for the opening.

The new museum building was completed by the summer of 1856 and arrangements for the Commissioners of Patents' Museum commenced, not without some misunderstandings. When Cole's Department of Science and Art wrote to Woodcroft in November requesting him to move the Commissioners to appoint "some person to communicate with the Department" he replied stiffly[26] that "the models in question were originally entrusted by their owners to my Personal care..."; he was responsible for their transfer, not the Patent Commissioners. This proprietorial tone was to cause tensions throughout the Museum's existence. He had delivered the models in February 1856 to temporary accommodation at Kensington Palace. The Museum arrangements were discussed by the Patent Commissioners on December 15 that year; Woodcroft was asked to be Superintendent, an arrangement confirmed by the Treasury the following January, not because he was to be paid additionally to his salary – he wasn't – but because the department kept an iron grip on even minor state appointments.

In the weeks leading up to the South Kensington Museum opening in June 1857 the new Superintendent quickly appointed staff[27]: the first and short-lived curator, George Nasmyth (a brother of the Manchester engineer and inventor James Nasmyth), a mechanical assistant W.H. Beck, at £80 p.a. and an attendant John Baskerville, at 3/6d a week. These were all in place before the end of February 1857, at a time when Cole and John Kelk were still testing colours for the interior decoration of the iron building.

The Museum had a series of openings[28]: the royal opening on Saturday, June 20, 1857, when the Queen "expressed herself quite pleased with all the arrangements" a private view for notables on a following evening, and the public opening on Wednesday, June 24. Students were present during the royal opening – it is easy to forget that the South Kensington complex was educational as well as a museum, with the Design School occupying some of the old Brompton House buildings as well as the new temporary ones.

The Patent Museum or "Museum and Library in connection with the Great Seal Patent Office" occupied only about a twelfth of the ground area of the "Boilers" at the South end in a central bay adjacent to the Educational Museum. It is not clear even from John Physick's very detailed history of the South Kensington buildings whether all eight sections of the Museum – apart from the Sheepshanks paintings – were in the iron "Boilers". One contemporary account of the opening describes it as a wing of the entire edifice, but certainly this "annexe" contained the major part of the collections: a modern sculpture collection, architectural casts and drawings, a circulating art library, the educational collection, another illustrating building, and the utilitarian-sounding "animal products".

Describing the public opening, *The Illustrated Times* referred to the Educational Collection as probably the most popular part of the whole exhibition, with the Patents Museum as "a sort of supplement".

121

The South Kensington Museum was open six days a week, with Wednesdays, Thursdays and Fridays as students days, when a 6d charge was made. Hours were: 10–4 but thanks to gas, on certain evenings it was kept open until 10, allegedly a "first" for a British public institution[29]. The press made much of the moral effect of this alternative to the gin shop. (The effect of gas on paintings was tested by some prominent scientists.) Woodcroft proudly reported that at first his catalogue was the only one available but this is contradicted by reports of a 1d catalogue. His may well have been the only one of substance.

In this setting for the next 27 years the Patent Museum survived somewhat precariously as a separately administered enclave within the main Museum. It had no regular acquisitions grant, only an allowance for operating costs and each acquisition had to be separately begged for from the Treasury, which usually refused. (In this it was no worse off than other institutions.) It was predictably unpopular with some officials; in 1858 Woodcroft told the Attorney General[30] that Bowring, of the Trade department would like to take it all over for the main Museum, and the Patent Office revenues too, but he may have been exaggerating. The Museum was plagued with uncertainty as to accommodation. Nevertheless it was popular with visitors, and despite press exaggeration of differences with the Director, Henry Cole, the two institutions managed to coexist and to some extent cooperate. If they had not, conditions would have been impossible. Above all, as Superintendent, Woodcroft, though short of resources, was in a good position to indulge his ruling trait, that of the romantic antiquarian, a Schliemann of historic machinery.

Visiting the Museum immediately after the opening, *The Mechanics' Magazine* reported[31] it as:

> ...well worth the attention of the inventive and scientific portion of our readers. The most prominent model is Symington's patent marine steam engine... this will form an attraction as long as it exists. Besides this, there are a hundred other models of various kinds, a very large number of which have been contributed by Mr Woodcroft to whose zeal the public is indebted for the creditable and interesting character of the Museum.

The same journal's account[32] after a pre-opening view suggests that Woodcroft was attempting a rational arrangement even at this early stage:

> We are gratified to observe that Mr Woodcroft is very wisely endeavouring to bring together in this Museum models classified and arranged in such a manner as to tell the historical tale of the gradual improvement of each branch of practical art and manufacture...

This was more an endeavour than an accomplishment, on the evidence of the now rare early catalogues[33] of the collection. In its third year (1859) it numbered over 300 exhibits, ranging from artefacts that have become national treasures to a fringe including an ancient British funeral urn and some Roman pottery, both lent by the Superintendent. There is some justification for the claim in the steam engines and components, the textile machinery (including many of Bodmer's inventions), and marine propellers. Most were serious and patented inventions. A feature of the earliest catalogues is the substantial history and description of important exhibits. By 1863 the collection had trebled in size, suggesting an enthusiastic response from inventors and others.

At times it was over-enthusiastic: when offered a picture entitled "Elves and Fairies" Woodcroft replied politely, "I would be very glad to receive it if it were connected with invention". (In a sense it was.)

Some thought that patented inventions only were admissible, and others supposed that being a patentee entitled them to a place; both were wrong.

The character of the Patent Museum and its contribution to the national collections during its relatively brief independent life were defined just as that life was ending in the report of a Treasury Inter-Departmental Committee[34] chaired by the civil engineer Sir Frederick Bramwell:

> The title "Patent Museum" was never accurate: the collection might with greater propriety have been called the 'Woodcroft Museum' from the name of the gentleman, formerly clerk to the Commissioners of Patents who originated the formation of it. It contains objects illustrating steps in the history of mechanical inventions, and contrivances of importance and interest, regardless of whether they have been patented or not.

A sub-committee – it included heavyweights such as Sir William Armstrong and Joseph Bazalgette, the father of the London sewers, specially considering the mechanical collections concluded by suggesting the preservation of some few very old machines[35] of great historical interest, naming "Watt's first engine, Trevithick's locomotive and Stationary engines, Stephenson's *Rocket* and Hackworth's *Sans Pareil* and *Puffing Billy* locomotives..."

It was unfair that Woodcroft (who died in 1879) was unable to read these words (a tribute the Patent Office never paid him in its own reports), which will serve to preface a brief account of this eminently "heritage" operation. Superimposed on the Museum's daily function of entertaining and instructing the South Kensington crowds was the intermittent minor drama of important acquisitions, usually on a fiscal shoestring. The committee did not mention the Symington marine engine, the engine of Henry Bell's *Comet* steamboat, Patrick Bell's reaper, the Dover Castle and Wells Cathedral clocks, and Arkwright's prototype spinning frame. The story of recovery is only fitfully illuminated in the surviving primary records.

The Symington engine, Woodcroft's favourite "parent engine of steam navigation"[36] is, for this reason, one of the best documented. It was recovered and kept at the Patent Office before the Museum opened in 1857. It was a product of the ferment of invention and industrial activity in Scotland at the end of the 18th century. The Edinburgh banker and restless improver Patrick Miller[37] (1731-1815) – he also experimented with new crops and is credited with inventing the Carronade naval gun – became interested in ship propulsion. After experiments with man-powered paddle craft he commissioned William Symington (1763-1831), engineer at the Leadhills mines, to build a twin-cylinder atmospheric steam engine to be installed in a small catamaran-type boat. On a now legendary occasion, October 14, 1788, it was tested on Miller's private lake at Dalswinton, Dumfriesshire. The trial, however controversial its outcome, had several appealing features: it was a first for this side of the Atlantic, it was remote, it was a quasi-domestic occasion attended by the local tenantry, including Robert Burns and was painted by Alexander Nasmyth[38].

Miller did not persist with steamboats; his offer to collaborate with Watt and Boulton met with a crushing negative; Watt, the supreme

124

professional did not approve of amateurs, but his experiments and Symington's later work influenced Henry Bell, and Fulton in America. After display at Dalswinton House, Symington's engine began the wandering[39] that was to end at the Patent Museum. It was sent to Coutt's Bank in London, then to a Marylebone store, after which track of it was lost for a time.

Woodcroft studied the Miller case in detail for his *Sketch of the Origin and Progress of Steam Navigation* and illustrated it with Nasmyth's painting (re-drawn by the distinguished railway artist J.C. Bourne and lithographed) but his hunt for the engine did not begin until his first year at the Patent Office. Busy with arranging the printing of the patents (see above) in March 1853 he commissioned an agent in Edinburgh, Richard Telford[40], to make enquiries.

It had been sold as scrap to William Kirkwood and Sons, plumber and gasfitter of West Thistle St, North Lane, Edinburgh, where Telford, after clearance from Woodcroft, bought it for £7 and despatched it to London "per luggage train, Caledonian Railway", on the 19th of April. Telford's final report gave a few details of the search:

Millers Engine

My dear Sir,

Now to answer your several questions.-

The engine came into Mr Mackenzie's possession on the 3rd of February 1846 where it remained some time, but being much in his way and not conceiving it to be of any use (for he thought it to be a model of some description of pump) he sent it for storage to Mr Peter S. Fraser Agent to the United Kingdom Insurance Co, George St, Edinburgh where it remained for some time, when he instructed Mr Fraser to sell it for what it might be worth, that gentleman accordingly sold it *framing and all as described in your book* on the 6th of July 1848 to his Brother in law, the late Mr William Kirkwood, Plumber, Thistle St Lane, Edinburgh for the sum of £2.12.8 (I copied the entry myself from Mr Kirkwood's ledger) who disengaged it from its framing and threw it in a corner for the purpose of melting and where I found all the parts forwarded by me to you. I believe I have now fully answered all your questions. You of course are at liberty to make use of this information in any way you please.

Through ignorance of their historic importance, the ferrous parts of the engine comprising Symington's complicated transmission system and engine mounting were thus lost.

What remained of the engine was handed over to the marine engineers John Penn and Son, of Greenwich, for "reinstatement", virtually a re-creation round the original brass cylinders and pistons; their detailed description of the work[41], running to several pages of manuscript, leaves no doubt as to the scale of the reconstruction. They waived the cost, £257 (perhaps £12,000 now) as a gift to the nation. In the summer of 1854 Woodcroft made a pilgrimage to Dalswinton[42] and made fragmentary notes of the recollections of older residents but they leave intact the mystery of the boat's performance. The restored engine went to the Patent Museum in January 1857. *The Mechanics' Magazine* published a detailed account of its odyssey, authoritative, as it was supplied by Woodcroft himself. Assiduous always, he checked with Lord Brougham himself, an account that stated that the future Chancellor, was among the passengers, who refuted it, but mentioned that he had witnessed other experiments by Miller as a child.

Recent experts have questioned that the engine could have propelled a boat at the 5 mph claimed in the early reports. A test run of the reconstructed engine would surely have been an event; in a letter to *The Engineer* in 1876, John Penn claimed that it *had* been run, by steam. This "parent engine" had no direct progeny.

The Museum's contribution to the national collection of James Watt's inventions was particularly notable. His "cabinet" (small or workshop) steam engine was bequeathed to John Kennedy, a Manchester textile engineer, and passed to his grandson, Albert Greg or Greig; there is a letter of May 1858 from Edwin Chadwick[43] to Gipps at the Museum, stating it was in Greig's possession. It was first lent to the Museum the same year. Two important donations[44] followed in 1861: the Birmingham firm Branson and Gwyther presented some substantial remains of the earliest industrial engine carrying Watt's improvements, "Old Bess", used to pump water for driving machinery by water wheel at the Soho Works in Birmingham. The same year, 1861, Boulton's grandson Matthew Piers Watt Boulton bequeathed a complete beam engine embodying some of Watt's most elegant mechanisms, the sun-and-planet gear and "parallel motion", the latter a linkage for accommodating the arc of the pivoted beam to the reciprocating piston rod. This "lap" engine of 1788 drove polishing machinery in the production of metalwares at Soho.

Attempts to acquire the contents of Watt's home workshop, the famous sealed garret and to reproduce it in London were made by Woodcroft from 1864 to the 1870s. It was a situation made for him. On Watt's death in 1819 his son James left Heathfield House to be occupied by his married niece Mrs Gibson, but reverentially sealed the garret where his father had experimented. The house was inherited by her son, J.W.Gibson Watt, and let. The workshop remained locked for 45 years. The prestige of a national museum persuaded the family to allow it to be opened, with the agreement of their solicitor Richard Banks, on the 4th of May, 1864. Woodcroft described the occasion in a letter to Sir John Romilly[45], the Master of the Rolls:

> The Birmingham *savans* have solicited in vain to be allowed to look into this chamber. Mr Smith [the curator] and myself are the first persons, I believe, who were ever permitted to enter this room and I attribute this especial favour to the circumstance of our having collected so goodly a number of the relics of Watt ...

Some reports state that Samuel Smiles was present, but Woodcroft does not mention him:

> Mr Pemberton (the tenant), his wife and daughters and a lady visitor, Miss Gibson, her brother, Mr Watt, Mr Smith and myself were the party now ready to face the stratum of dust that had been collecting since the year 1819. Mr Watt, had he been a superstitious man, might have sent us home with a good excuse for the door refused to be opened until after a twenty minute struggle with it ...

> On entering the room we found everything most systematically arranged. Under the window was fixed the turning lathe, on the left a machine to carve a small bust from a large one. On the right was a machine for carving medallions. In drawers we found splendid works of art carved by these machines and produced in a variety of substances from Marble, mother of pearl, to common deal.

127

Woodcroft wanted to recreate the room round the original contents, in London; a few days after the opening he requested permission[46] from the solicitor to have a drawing made of the interior. In 1866 he told the younger Watt[47] that a fireproof room already called the Watt room was available at the Holborn office. He wrote again in 1872, "there is one eminently fitted to exhibit them in this office[48]. When a new library and other offices were added to this building I had a room specially provided for that collection and gave it the name of Watt's room". (He was alluding to the Pennethorne extension of 1867.) Not for the last time he was frustrated, but his aim was realised in this century at the Science Museum. In 1876, too, one of the two museums acquired some of Watt's experimental apparatus, notably condensers, from the family.

The most extreme example of Woodcroft's collecting enthusiasm concerned the putative steam engine of the 2nd Marquis of Worcester (1601-1667). On the evidence of the Marquis' statement that a model of the engine would be buried with him, he got the consent of the church authorities[49] and the Beaufort estates to break into the family vault of the Somersets in Raglan church, Monmouthshire, and cut open the lead coffins of the Marquis and others. His accomplice on this escapade was John Macgregor. They found no model or drawing. It is best savoured in Macgregor's account with sketches now in the Science Museum.

Of the two steam locomotives, *Rocket* and *Puffing Billy*[50], the stars of the Museum's collection, *Rocket* was acquired first. It had been built in 1829 by Robert Stephenson & Co., for the Liverpool and Manchester Railway. It was winner of the famous Rainhill trials the same year. *Rocket* retired from working life in 1844 and was offered for showing in the 1851 Exhibition but was refused. The British Museum also refused it a home. In 1862 it was donated to the Museum by Thompson and Sons of Kirkhouse, near Carlisle, after correspondence with Pettit Smith the curator.

Puffing Billy was built in 1813 to haul coal from Wylam Colliery in Northumberland to the staithe at Lemington-on-Tyne and was not retired until 1862. In 1864 the owner, Edward Blackett, evidently hoped[51] the Museum would buy it; there is a letter (from the Army and Navy Club) in which he asks £1,200 for it, adding "More I do not think of asking" and suggesting that the Commissioners' dignity would prevent them offering less. The Treasury had no dignity in such matters and the locomotive was probably at first lent and later donated. The authenticity of both engines was sometimes questioned, but alterations to the original design were inevitable in such long working lives.

The search for important artefacts and dealings with potential contributors sometimes illuminated the insecurity of life in the 19th century, even in such a profession as engineering. The engine of Henry Bell's *Comet*, which powered the first short-lived steamboat passenger service in 1812, had begun life as a workshop engine and after being salvaged returned to stationary duty. In July 1864 the firm of G. Allan and Son, Clyde Forge Rivet Foundry, reported to the naval architect John Scott Russell[52] that the engine was at a works in Rutherglen (north-west Lanark):

> With regard to the boiler, we had it lying outside our gate for 3 or 4 years, but it was eating itself up and much in our way, and we sent it the way of all scrap. No doubt a great piece of vandalism... The old man that made the engine is still in Glasgow in very destitute circumstances.

This vignette was happily not the final one: John Robertson the engine builder was enabled by the donor of the engine, the marine engineer and shipbuilder Robert Napier, to come to the Museum and superintend its mounting for display.

Scott Russell as a Great Exhibition commissioner, important member of the Society of Arts and shipbuilder was of Woodcroft's milieu and a friend. He had donated a model of the giant paddle engines of *The Great Eastern* to the Museum. In 1870 just before the outbreak of the Franco-Prussian War he was working on a project with the French Government. From the Hotel Bristol in Paris, he wrote to reclaim the model[53] for sale:

> I really want the money – I hope your organisations at the Patent Office go on to your mind – the Public has been greatly benefited by your exertions – whether the Public will ever show you any gratitude is quite another question.

The model did eventually remain in the Museum.

The Wells Cathedral clock is one of the very earliest European mechanical clocks; first reference to a "clokk" in the cathedral account rolls is in the year 1392/3. It has an elaborate astronomical dial showing the age and phases of the moon, mechanical figures performing the chiming and striking, and an hourly carousel of jousting horsemen. In 1837 a new movement was made by the Clerkenwell firm of Thwaites and Reed, the original, now a cherished exhibit at the Science Museum, was stored in an undercroft. In August 1871, Pettit Smith reported[54] in unbuttoned style to his assistant on his mission to acquire it for the Patent Museum:

> I yesterday fired off two big canons, one minor do and two small arms beside the Bishop. The Rev. Mr Keene to whom my introductory letter was addressed has left Wells several years since. His successor, Rev. Mr Beresford is out on his holidays, his curate Mr Martyn opened my letters & kindly came to my aid and took me straight away to the cathedral in order to lay hold of the Bishop as soon as the service was over. We followed his "Lordship" home to his palace and were introduced immediately, had a long "confab" with him. I have been invited by my friend the Curate to join a "Pic–Nic" at 11 a.m. today at the Cheddar cliffs where I shall meet all the Big Guns and small arms and a six shooter or two and maybe shall further my object more or less by mixing with that lot.

The Chapter agreed[55] to lend the clock, at first for two years. By November 1871 it was on private view at South Kensington. In 1874 they asked for it back, but, like the paddle engine model it eventually joined the permanent collection. A pit was dug – with Office of Works permission – to allow for the descent of the weights.

The Treasury treated the Museum, as it did most public projects, with consistent meanness. It provided a small annual grant for operating costs but no acquisitions budget; each application to purchase had to be made individually and was usually refused. In 1870, Woodcroft was offered a Newcomen engine[56] from the famous Carron foundry in Scotland. He arranged storage at a naval yard and asked, as he usually did, for free rail transport from the Great Northern Railway, which was refused. Transport by sea was considered but the Treasury refused any grant and the engine never came to London. In 1868 Woodcroft acquired Patrick Bell's reaping machine, the first successful British machine; it was pushed by horses rather than pulled. As Mrs Bell was still using it, a replacement had to be supplied[57]. She cannily asked for a state-of-the-art 2-horse machine which Woodcroft paid for himself. Several years later the Treasury reluctantly paid[58] £28.15s to allow Bell's reaper to remain in the Museum; it was among the exhibits Woodcroft considered as his own. The Treasury also refused £52.10s for the restoration of the dial of the Wells clock, though it did grant a smaller sum for the work on the movement. In 1872 the Attorney General, J.D. Coleridge, in a rare intervention by a patent commissioner, commented on the Treasury's refusal of £120[59] for Museum improvements. Whenever possible Woodcroft disguised the cost of restoration work in the household budget.

In the later years of the Museum under the Commissioners the Treasury began to dictate policy more sternly: in 1876 the many-sided W.H. Smith II, then Secretary to the Treasury, instructed the Commissioners that "the Museum should be strictly what its name implies, viz. a Museum of Patented Inventions, and that even of these, only models should be admitted, while all other articles however interesting should be rejected"[60]. The Museum was to be strictly a branch of the Office. This was the conclusion of an unpublished enquiry by Smith and Sir George Jessel, the Master of the Rolls. Its secrecy and its conclusions, which Smith let slip in Parliament, were criticised in the journal *Engineering*[61], which pointed out that the Museum already far exceeded Smith's prescription. It added that the models in the US Patent Office were of little or no value.

The Treasury's policy was often reiterated; fortunately the Museum for much of its existence had not been bound by it. Some Treasury concern however, is understandable, as its cramped conditions were well known.

The Museum was dogged by uncertainty about accommodation throughout its existence; the evidence suggests that the Committee of Council for Education, controlling the South Kensington Museum, and the Treasury, would have been glad to see this troublesome enclave with its zealot Superintendent, absorbed into the main Museum. Trouble arose soon after the opening over the still controversial question of charges, and Woodcroft's insistence that the collection should be shown free of all charge. Entry was through an iron and glass conservatory-like structure at the south end of the "Boilers". (It had been added to relieve the

131

brutality of the building.) This meant that visitors to the Patent Museum had to pay Henry Cole's sixpence on three days a week. Woodcroft soon informed the Patent Commissioners that the terms of loan were being breached. He characteristically told the press too. *The Engineer* took an extreme view[62], accusing Cole of having deceived the Patent Museum over admission charges. The usually aloof Patent Commissioners were sympathetic to Woodcroft's stand, or were won over. Under their authority he issued a printed notice stating that the models would be removed unless they could be shown free. The Master of the Rolls had a meeting[63] with Prince Albert in March 1858; the Consort's wish was that the exhibits should not be moved and that Woodcroft (as he himself recorded it "should not be interfered with"). A separate entrance was made through a curious cottage-like structure on the south-west corner of the "Boilers". The triumphalist sign Museum of Patents, Entrance Free Daily can be seen in drawings of the "Boilers".

Whether it was a genuine triumph is another matter. The South Kensington authorities pointed out reasonably that the Patent Museum was losing the thousands of visitors who would have included it in their visit had not the two museums been separated internally. Cole made the point[64] at the 1864 enquiry on the Library and Museum. The charge was small and only on certain days.

On a more harmonious note, the two museums co-operated amicably when opened in the evenings for private views as they did for MPs in June 1858, and annually for the Society of Arts *conversazioni*.

The cause of the Museum's insecurity for much of its existence was the dismantling of a large part of the "Boilers" to build the Bethnal Green Museum. For several years of this creative period for museums there had been plans to establish several satellite institutions in the outer London districts. Land had been bought at Bethnal Green through the generosity of various donors, including Baroness Burdett-Coutts. In late 1864 and 1865 two-thirds of the "Boilers" were taken down and transported to Bethnal Green, leaving the Patent Museum islanded in the southern bay. The empty site was occupied by the gaunt Architectural Courts of the main Museum.

This was a good opportunity for the Science and Art Department to take over the Patent Museum, and in May 1865 Earl Granville, the Lord

President, proposed[65] this, offering Woodcroft space in the Arcades overlooking the Horticultural Society's gardens on the West side of Exhibition Road. These, with their flanking galleries, had formed part of the 1862 Exhibition buildings. (The site is where the Geological Museum and Science Museum now stand.) The Patent Commissioners met in crisis mode to consider the proposal. Woodcroft inspected the site[66] and thought it satisfactory. In June the Lord Chancellor's secretary, A.B. Abraham, wrote to Granville[67] concerning the conditions of transfer; free access was a *sine qua non*. Cole replied to Woodcroft, rather in the manner of "come in to my parlour..." that conditions would be exactly as for other lenders to the Museum, but that free access would be assured.

In July the vacation was looming and Cole agreed that the question could be shelved. In December Woodcroft was still worried about control, should they move to the Arcades. During the summer he had been offered space by the company[68] developing the Crystal Palace as a pleasure ground and musical centre at Sydenham. The Secretary was George Grove and Scott Russell, ever adventurous, was a partner. There is no record of the terms involved. Woodcroft delayed any decision

For the time no move took place. The Patent Museum remained in the draughty, leak-prone[69] rump of the "Boilers". There was some redecoration[70], and any space vacated by the South Kensington Museum was taken over. There were particular complaints about the small library space, 600 sq ft exposed at the north end of the building. As described (see Ch. 9) the Commons enquiry of 1864 had been illuminating but without result for the Museum.

In the 1870s the Exhibition Commissioners made another offer[71] of accommodation; this was of part of the remaining galleries of the 1862 International Exhibition on the south side of the Horticultural Gardens west of Exhibition Rd; the space could be bought for £30,000 or rented for £1,500. In March 1876 the Treasury was prepared to agree[72] that it could be shared with the National Portrait Gallery which still had no permanent home. Woodcroft, within days of his unheralded resignation, pressed for acceptance. One advantage, he stressed, would be space for the ever-growing bulk of printed specifications now filling a rented warehouse in Cursitor St. The Prussian Patent Office, he added, had donated "a large number of scientific works of folio size" for which there was no space. (Some of these were pattern books for decorators *GebrauchsMuster für Zimmerleute*, issued by the *Königlich Kaiserlich Deputation für Gewerbe* and are now in the British Library.) He also reported that the Museum needed weeding[73] of machines and models "useless in an educational point of view". For some reason, probably general official reluctance and the uncertainty as to the science collections as a whole – the move never took place.

The curators

The four Museum curators were strikingly diverse characters and exemplify the informality of museum life at the time; it seems few such posts, though in the public service, were advertised. The first, George Nasmyth, who was appointed for the initial setting up of the Museum in early 1857 was, as noted, a brother of James Nasmyth the inventor and owner of the notable Bridgwater armament works at Patricroft, Manchester. The warm friendship between James and Woodcroft almost certainly brought about the appointment. George Nasmyth handled some early acquisitions but in September 1859 he was suspended[74] "on suspicion of appropriating to his own use the public money intrusted to him". This was confirmed by an accountant and he was dismissed by order of the Commissioners after the Long Vacation. The following year Edmunds reported him[75] as having gone to America. "I have ascertained that although connected in near kindred with wealthy men, he did not at that time possess property nor is he likely at any time to possess property of any description".

1860 was a vexed year for the curatorship. Before Nasmyth's actual dismissal Woodcroft alerted two of his friends as to the possible vacancy; they were the Manchester machinist and consulting engineer Benjamin Fothergill, and Francis Pettit Smith, a national celebrity for his work in developing and fostering acceptance of the marine propeller. (At a public dinner and presentation of plate to Pettit Smith, Woodcroft was toasted with him as fellow pioneer.) The latter had approached Fothergill[76] to be the first curator, but as Woodcroft explained to the Commissioners when doubting that he would accept this second offer, he had asked for too large a salary.

Woodcroft told the Commissioners that, despite his regard for Pettit Smith, he favoured Fothergill[77] for his superior mechanical knowledge – he was a professional which, despite his achievement, Smith was not – but asked not to have to express his view openly as both men were friends. Pettit Smith had compiled a quite glittering memorial (i.e. testimonial) carrying the names of most of the greatest engineers of the period.

Despite Woodcroft's doubts, he had his preference and Fothergill was appointed[78] in April 1860 at a salary of £400, £100 more than Nasmyth.

By mid-July he announced that he wanted to resign[79], on the grounds that the conditions in the iron building made it impossible to do his job as responsible curator. At first Woodcroft with characteristic volatility thought they would be better without such petulant men, then changed his mind; Fothergill's complaint confirmed the unsuitability of the building.

Fothergill remained firm, and after many memos on the procedure for resigning such a post, he left in August. (He had already begun to take up consultancy work despite signing a declaration not to.) His resignation may have been a disastrous move, as within a few years he was ill in reduced circumstances.

Pettit Smith's appointment suggests how much coveted even such a relatively minor public post could be, though its nature in this instance specially appealed to him. As soon as Fothergill's departure was certain there were urgent exchanges between London and Frogmore[80], Guernsey, where Pettit Smith was at home on his farm. (In one letter he urged a reply by "electric message".) He had to agree to take the post without salary, as the Commissioners were on Long Vacation, and trust that his appointment would be approved. After a flying visit to London to meet Marwick Michell who was standing in as Curator he returned to precipitately sell his farm and – as he put it –"commence a new and I trust one of the most agreeable phases of my chequered career". Had he known more of conditions in the iron building he might have been less optimistic, but he held the post for nearly fourteen years until his death in 1874. He was knighted in 1871. If this was not galling to his superior and fellow inventor, Woodcroft must have been exceptionally magnanimous.

A very interesting aspect of this year of appointments is that it shows Woodcroft and Edmunds working apparently amicably together, agreeing arrangements for absences from the library (in one instance both attending "the great gun experiments" at Southport in July 1860) and Woodcroft acknowledging Edmunds as "my senior and superior in office". This was the man he would later charge with being absent from the office for months at a time.

Many of the Museum's most famous artefacts, such as *Rocket* and *Puffing Billy*, the *Comet* engine, Patrick Bell's reaper and the Wells Cathedral and Dover Castle clocks were acquired during Pettit Smith's curatorship. In 1862 he was assiduously following possible leads to surviving machines of Richard Trevithick[81] without success; the next curator was more fortunate.

Just how his successor was appointed is not clear. Lieutenant Colonel Archibald Henry Plantagenet Stuart Wortley[82] became curator in June 1874. He is distinctive among Patent Office staff for his titled connections and it seems unlikely that he was a nominee of Woodcroft's. His father was the second son of the 1st Baron Wharncliffe, and his mother, Lady Emmeline Charlotte Stuart Wortley was a daughter of the 5th Duke of Rutland and was a poet and travel writer. His sister Victoria, Lady Welby Gregory, was a linguist and philosopher. Stuart Wortley had been MP for Honiton. He is best-known now as a photographer. He was an important member of the Photographic Society of London, and in 1864 set up a limited company, the United Association of Photography which patented a photographic printing process called the "Wothlytype" (a name derived not from his, but from its foreign inventor). The company was dissolved before he came to the Museum. His work is still collected and exhibited. The arrival of such a young and well connected subordinate – he was in his early forties, was evidently not welcome to Woodcroft now in his 70s.

He evidently saw himself as a badly needed new broom, a view shared by some of the technical press, though with misgivings. The journal *Engineering* hoped[83] that the new curator would apply his "admitted administrative capacity" to the disgraceful condition of the collection, a result of Woodcroft's miserable policy of masterly inactivity". Later, in 1876, after Woodcroft had retired, Stuart Wortley wrote: "all this extra work is rendered necessary by the fact that Mr Woodcroft never allowed cleaning[84] or rearrangement, though frequently pressed by me". After

136

Woodcroft's achievements this comes as a shock and is perhaps linked to the circumstances of his health and sudden retirement.

Stuart Wortley's administrative experience is confirmed by a crisp management style. He initiated or presided over more important acquisitions. In 1876 the Museum acquired Arkwright's original spinning frame[85]; it was owned by Benjamin Fothergill and had been lent to the Peel Park Museum at Salford. Perhaps because of the prestige of Arkwright's name but more probably because it was small, the Treasury agreed to pay £75 to acquire it for the nation. He tried but failed to acquire a Harrison chronometer at a sale. In 1878 he proposed that the Museum be lit by "the electric light" from a local generator[86]. At this time officials of the South Kensington Museum, were investigating electric lighting as was the War Office. In 1879 a stationary agricultural steam engine designed by Richard Trevithick was exhibited at the Agricultural Society's exhibition and Stuart Wortley suggested acquiring it before it was returned to its owner, Sir C. Hawkins, of "Trewithen", Grampound Road, in Cornwall. As in the case of the Bell reaper, this still-in-service engine was exchanged[87] for a more up to date one. The Treasury refused extra funds, but the Master of the Rolls was in favour[88] and the money was found. In pressing for this exchange Stuart Wortley called the Museum the "scientific museum of the country".

To its own temporary impoverishment, it contributed to the most important scientific exhibition of the century, the Loan Exhibition of Scientific Apparatus (a broadly interpreted title) mounted by the South Kensington Museum. It opened in May 1876. Organised by a large international committee[89] (Woodcroft was on the Mechanical section) and in keeping with the educational character of the South Kensington institutions, it was primarily to instruct rather than delight; the arrangement of machines and instruments from several European countries was strictly classified. It was mounted in the Galleries on the West side of Exhibition Road. The Patent Museum lent the two famous locomotives, the Symington engine, the Bell reaper and a steam hammer. The exhibition resulted in now historically valuable accounts[90] and illustrations of these and other machines in the press. There were complaints that the public now had to pay to see them.

Woodcroft's retirement in March 1876 resulted in a long-running dispute over the ownership of machines and models, portraits and books which ended only with his wife's bequest to the South Kensington Museum in 1903. Understandably though (it now seems) misguidedly, he could not give up a proprietary interest in the collections he had created. In May 1876, Stuart Wortley reported, "Mr Woodcroft is here daily"[91]. Wortley had agreed with the South Kensington authorities that large machines such as the locomotives should remain[92] in the Galleries after the Loan Exhibition. The Symington engine and some others were shown as lent by Woodcroft. Stuart Wortley requested their return[93] to his museum, "Mr Woodcroft should not have put them in his name"; the South Kensington management had undertaken to return them to their owners and duly delivered them to his home. During the following two years the removal of more of the collection was recorded punctiliously: in 1878 Lack – now head of the Office – reported that Woodcroft had removed[94] by agreement over 200 portraits, medallions and busts, over 50 engineering drawings and over 60 models, while more were claimed and being investigated. (In this, Woodcroft's excellent records were essential.) Lack investigated the ownership[95] of the Symington engine and concluded that it was the property of the nation on the strength of Penn's gratis work of restoration. This case, now called *Patent Office v. Woodcroft*[96], was submitted to the Law Officers, who decided otherwise, and the engine was not returned. At this time Miller's grandson[97], Colonel W.H. Miller, who was attempting a life of his grandfather, visited the Museum claiming mistakenly that the latter had himself donated it.

Fortunately for the Museum, many of its most important items were not in dispute. Unfortunately for Woodcroft, a more efficient reaper than Bell's was in contention, he died in February 1879 leaving all his real and personal property including material in the Patent Office and Museum, to his wife, Agnes Bertha Woodcroft. Almost immediately she had the collections valued and began negotiations[98] with the Patent Office, offering for sale not only machines, models, portraits from the Gallery of Inventors and books, but also *objets d'art* from her husband's collection. Relevant items were chosen, including £50 worth of books for the Patent Office Library, but many were rejected. The Symington engine was valued at £800 but was evidently not bought, as it is missing from a handbill of the early 1880's, listing the star exhibits.

For many years official and scientific opinion had been moving in favour of amalgamation of the best of the Patent Museum with the national science and engineering collection at South Kensington. A number of witnesses at the 1871/2 Patent Law enquiry had seen a museum as a necessary adjunct of the Patent Office as in the US, but the existing museum had outstripped this conception. Woodcroft's was an increasingly lone voice[99] before his retirement; he claimed that models might be wanted at short notice by litigating patentees. Transfer to another authority would be unfair to the staff, including himself. In 1876, too, the then Master of the Rolls still thought that the Museum should stay with the Office.

Surprisingly, the 1871/2 enquiry (see Ch. 9) ignored the Museum in its report. A significant development took place in 1876; a powerful memorial[100] headed by the name of J.D. Hooker, President of the Royal Society, signed by scores of prominent engineers and scientists in favour of a museum of pure and applied science to include the Patent Museum, was addressed to the Lord President (the Duke of Richmond and Gordon). "We are of opinion that, as standing alone, and purely as subjects of a patent, their value is far less than if they formed part of a general collection". The petition cited a report of the Royal Commission for Scientific Instruction recommending the uniting of the South Kensington collections under a single authority and in a new building. Thus the Science Museum was conceived, but it would be many years and committees before it was born.

Meanwhile the Patent Museum was interfering with the South Kensington Museum's building plans: the latter wanted the remains of the "Boilers"[101] for its South Eastern galleries. In 1882 the Treasury pointed out that funds for building depended[102] on legislation authorising the absorption of the Patent Museum and its removal. A brief clause in the 1883 Patents Act transferring the Patent Office to the Board of Trade (see Ch. 11) finally vested the vexed collection in the South Kensington Museum.

Stuart Wortley had seen for some time that his future lay in that direction. In October 1883, when the Act was law, he wrote to Sir John Donnelly[103], Cole's successor, "I saw Mr Lack (now head of the Patent Office) yesterday. But I gathered from him that as the Museum is transferred to you by *Act of Parliament* and that the same Act abolishes the Commissioners of Patents and their Clerk (himself) the moribund Commissioners can hardly assume the right of giving you what you already possess".

He concludes archly, "But could you not write and ask him for salaries and services of the employes (sic) here, and if he recommends any for employment in your Department".

Donnelly complied, and he supplied a militarily terse confidential report[104] on the staff now risen to eleven: four craftsmen, four attendants, a boy messenger and a charlady, besides the deputy curator. Mr Hunt, attendant and an ex-dragoon came in for special praise as a cleaner of "bright work". Wortley then recommended himself[105] to Sir Philip Cunliffe Owen, the director of collections, for a rise on the grounds of a frozen salary for seven years. "I think therefore that your kind interference to place the head of your scientific collections at £600 will no doubt be granted". When the Treasury-Bramwell Committee[106] on the national science collections (referred to above) reported in 1885 the Patent Museum collection, now part of the South Kensington Museum, was still in the iron building on the east side of Exhibition Road. When a second Treasury report appeared in 1889, the collection had at last moved west to the South Galleries proposed so many years earlier. Such were the delays in the progress of what eventually became the Victoria and Albert Museum and the Science Museum that the remains of the "Boilers" were still standing in the 1890s, with the entrance to the Patent Museum still forlornly visible.

Stuart Wortley had his wish, and became head of the engineering and science collection of what was still the South Kensington Museum. He became ill in 1888 and died the following year at his home, Rosslyn House, Grove End Rd in St John's Wood.

Mrs Woodcroft died in 1903 – leaving a remarkable and redeeming will[107], leaving all Patent Museum–related property ("portraits, models, machines") to the trustees of the South Kensington Museum. This was when that emblem of Woodcroft's lasting achievement (but also of his cussedness) the Symington engine – if not lent earlier – returned to the Museum. The bequest included "autographs and manuscripts relating to inventors" some or all of which came to the Patent Office Library. It also included Woodcroft's antiques collection, "paintings, pictures, framed prints and engravings, metal ware, bronzes, old furniture and glass". Rejected items, including bric-a-brac which had been in the Patent Museum were sold by Foster's, of Pall Mall; the chosen items, form the Woodcroft Bequest in the Victoria and Albert and Science Museums.

140

Notes to Chapter 13

1 HRH questioned   Royal Archives Minute, 29.12.1852.
   Professor Woodcroft

2 met the Prince Consort   Ibid, Letter, Woodcroft to Col.Phipps, 10.1. 1853.
   again

3 in late January was in   Ibid, Letter, Woodcroft to Col.Phipps, 21.1. 1853.
   touch

4 to petition   BLSRIS SC, collection of petitions (copy).

5 attempting to cancel   Royal Archives, Woodcroft to Phipps, 5.2.1853.

6 Their Supplemental   Commissioners for the Exhibition of 1851, 2nd
   Charter   Report, p.6,7.

7 The admirable effects   Ibid.
   produced

8 They set up a special   Ibid, 3rd Report, 1856, p.35.
   committee

9 The Commissioners   Ibid.
   (of Patents) are taking

10 one of his referees   University College London, Record Office and Library,
   wrote   John Graham to C.C. Atkinson, 1847?

11 thirty cases   Harrison, J. *Bennet Woodcroft at the Society of Arts,
                1845-57*.III. RSA Journal, 1982, p.375.

12 many "supernumerary"   Wood, H.T. *The History of the Royal Society of Arts*,
                London, Murray, 1913, p.381.

13 organise a collection   Woodcroft Collection, Appeal notice. Bodmer, BLSRIS
                SC.

14 dark corridors and rooms Harding, *Patent Office Centenary*, p.12.

15 wrote to E.A. Bowring   Commissioners for the Exhibition of 1851, Archive.
                Letter, 18.2.1854.

16 *The Birmingham Journal* 5. 3.1856.

17 Woodcroft has been   Commissioners for the Exhibition of 1851, 3rd Report,
   zealously engaged   p.36.

18 Gottfried Semper   Physick, *The Victoria and Albert Museum*, Oxford, 1982,
                pp.22, 23.

19 estimate for an "iron   Commissioners for the Exhibition of 1851, 3rd Report,
   building suited for a   Appendix T, pp.269, 270.
   museum"

20 a Museum of Patented Inventions — Ibid, p.271.

21 Sir William Cubitt accepted — Ibid, Archive, fol. 37.

22 iron-columned open-plan structure — Physick, p.23.

23 cast and wrought iron — Commission for the Exhibition of 1851 Archive, fol.39.

24 to alleviate the iron exterior — Physick, p.25.

25 The old decaying buildings — Ibid, pp.26-29.

26 he replied stiffly — Commission of the Exhibition of 1851, Archive. Woodcroft to? 24.11.1856.

27 quickly appointed staff — Patent Office, Staff Register.I.

28 a series of openings — Physick, p.38. *Illustrated Times*, 27.6.1857, pp.411.412.

29 allegedly a "first" — *Illustrated Times*, as cited.

30 Woodcroft told the Attorney General — letter, 10.3.1858, SML Z24-B 264.

31 *The Mechanics' Magazine* reported — **66**, 27.6.1857.

32 The same journal's account — **66**, 9.5.1857, p. 446

33 rare early catalogues — *Descriptive Catalogue of the Machines, Models etc. in the Museum of the Commissioners of Patents...3rd ed,1859.*

34 Treasury Inter-Departmental Committee — On the Scientific and Technical Collections at South Kensington. Report, 27.7.1885, p.9.

35 some few very old machines — Ibid, p.30.

36 parent engine of steam navigation — Catalogue, 1859 as cited, p.5.

37 Patrick Miller — Woodcroft Collection. BLSRIS SC. Includes original Milleriana.

38 painted by Alexander Nasmyth — BLSRIS SC, *Steam Navigation Papers*, Vol.1 James Nasmyth to Woodcroft, 4.10.1847, with "my father's sketch of Miller's double vessel".

39 Symington's engine began the wandering — *The Engineer*, **41**, 1876, pp.389-390 (on the Loan Exhibition at the South Kensington Museum, 1876).

40 an agent, Richard Telford — Telford to Woodcroft, 15.3.1853, to 26,4,1853. *Steam Navigation Papers*, 6, BLSRIS SC.

41 their detailed description of the work — Invoice, John Penn and Co., 1.12.1856, BLSRIS SC, *Steam Navigation Papers*, 5.

42 a pilgrimage to Dalswinton — Woodcroft Collection, Miller, BLSRIS SC.

43 letter…from Edwin Chadwick — 20.5.1858, SML Z 24–B.

44 Two important donations — South Kensington Museum, *Catalogue of Machinery Models, Etc*, 2nd ed. 1896: *The Science Museum, The First Hundred Years*, HMSO, 1957.

45 a letter to Sir John Romilly — 10.5.1864, Published in *The Engineer*, 8.6.1877, p.398.

46 he requested permission — Woodcroft to R. Banks, 27.5.1864. SML Z24–D (copy).

47 he told the younger Watt — Woodcroft to Gibson Watt, 7.11.1866, SML Z24–E (1148).

48 to exhibit them in this office — Woodcroft to Gibson Watt, 19.1.1872, SML Z24–G (1531).

49 the consent of the church authorities — BLSRIS SC, Woodcroft Collection Worcester file. Macgregor's account, with his sketches is in the SML. Hewish, J. *The Raid on Raglan*, BLJ 8, No 2,1982.

50 *Rocket* and *Puffing Billy* — South Kensington Museum, *Catalogue of Machines, Models, Etc.*, pt I,1896, nos 94,97. T.C. Thompson to F.P. Smith, 14.7.1862, SMLZ24–D (854).

51 Edward Blackett evidently hoped — Letter, 17.6.1864, SML Z24–D (995).

52 reported to the naval architect John Scott Russell — G. Allan to Russell, 17.6.1864, SML Z24–D. (876).

53 wrote to reclaim the model — Russell to Woodcroft (Mar/April 1870), SML Z24–F (1432,1434).

54 Pettit Smith reported — to J. Baskerville, 25.8.1871, SML Z24–G (1440).

55 The Chapter agreed — F.P. Smith to Woodcroft, 18.12.1872. SML Z24–G.

56 was offered a Newcomen engine — SML Z24–F (1420) (corresp. with Royal Victoria Yard, Woolwich).

57 a replacement had to be supplied — 10,11.11.1868, SML Z24–E corresp. Bells and F.P. Smith).

58 Treasury reluctantly paid — SML Z24–I (1841).

59 Treasury's refusal of £120 *The Globe*, 11.12.1872, SML Z24–G.

60 strictly what its name implies   W.H. Smith to Commissioners of Patents, 28.1.1876, SML Z24–H (1774).

61 criticised in the journal *Engineering*   Leader, 27, 2.6.1876, p.464.

62 *The Engineer* took an extreme view   24.7.1857.

63 The Master of the Rolls had a meeting   Woodcroft, *Minute Book*. Transcript. BLSRIS SC, Woodcroft file.

64 Cole made the point   Select Committee on the Patent Office Library and Museum. Minutes, Q.2309–2376.

65 Earl Granville, the Lord President, proposed   to Lord Chancellor, 16.5.1865, SML Z24–E.

66 Woodcroft inspected the site   Ibid, 8.6.1865.

67 Abraham wrote to Granville   Ibid, 17.6.1865.

68 offered space by the Company   Ibid, Woodcroft to G, Grove, 7.7.1865 (1115).

69 draughty, leak-prone   Ibid, F.P. Smith to Woodcroft, 13.12.1867 (1175).

70 some redecoration   Ibid, F.P.Smith to Woodcroft, 29.1.1868 (1187)

71 the Exhibition Commissioners made another offer   20.7.1874. SML Z24–G (1676).

72 Treasury was prepared to agree   to 1st Commissioner of Works, 13.3.1876, SML Z24–H.

73 Museum needed weeding   Woodcroft to W.H. Smith, 17.2.1875, SML Z24–H.

74 in 1859 he was suspended   Staff Register I.

75 Edmunds reported him   to Treasury, 14.3.1860, SMDC 37A–18 (copy)

76 The latter had approached Fothergill   Woodcroft to Sir. R. Bethell, 30.1.1860, SMDC 37A–18.

77 he favoured Fothergill   Ibid.

78 Fothergill was appointed   Ibid, Staff Register I.

79 he wanted to resign   Woodcroft to Fothergill, 14.8.1860 (copy) and to L. Edmunds, 19.7.1860, SMDC 37A–18.

80 Correspondence between 14.8.1860; 28.8.1860, SMDC 37A-18.
   London and Frogmore

81 surviving machines of Correspondence, Woodcroft, F.P. Smith, William
   Richard Trevithick Matthews, H.G. Haynes et al, 1862 1968, BLSRIS SC,
                       Woodcroft Coll.n, Trevithick.

82 Lt.Col. A.H.P. Stuart R.T. Smith to author, including information partly
   Wortley supplied by V. Dodier, V.&.A. Museum.

83 *Engineering* hoped 17, 4.1874, p.244.

84 Mr Woodcroft never S. Wortley to Lack, 12.1876, SML Z24-H (1816).
   allowed cleaning

85 acquired Arkwright's Ibid, Treasury to Lack, 25.8.76. (1812)
   original spinning frame

86 to be lit by "the electric S. Wortley to Lack, 18.12.1878, SML Z24-I (1882).
   light" Physick, pp.175,176.

87 still-in-service engine Stuart Wortley to Lack, 26.6.1879; Treasury to Lack,
   was exchanged 7.7.1879, SML Z24-I (1890).

88 the Master of the Rolls 28.7.1879, SML Z24 I (1895).
   was in favour

89 a large international Catalogue. South Kensington Museum, London, 1876.
   committee

90 historically valuable e.g. *The Engineer*, 1876, passim.
   accounts

91 "Mr Woodcroft is here Stuart Wortley to Lack, 11.3.1876, SML Z24-H.
   daily"

92 large machines such as Stuart Wortley to Cunliffe Owen, 25.9.1876, SML
   the locomotives should Z24-H (1815).
   remain

93 Stuart Wortley requested Ibid.
   their return

94 reported that Woodcroft Lack to Master of the Rolls, 22.6.1878, SML Z-30.
   had removed (copy).

95 Lack investigated the Lack to S.K. Museum, 9.7.1878, SML Z 24-I (1876).
   ownership

96 *Patent Office v. Woodcroft* Opinion, H.S. Giffard and John Holby, Attorney General
                       and Solicitor General. 22.5.1879, SMDC 77A5.

97 Miller's grandson Stuart Wortley to Lack, 8.8.1878, SML Z24-I (1881).

98 Mrs Woodcroft, SMDC, 77A6.
   negotiations

145

99 an increasingly lone voice   e.g. Woodcroft to LC. SMDC File 37, 4.2.1874, SML
                                  Z24–G.

100 a powerful memorial   Printed version, SMDC 37(i).

101 wanted the remains of   Physick, p.179.
    the Boilers

102 funds for building   L. Courtney, Treasury to Science and Art Department,
    depended   16.12.1882 (copy). SMDC, Science & Art 7015.

103 he wrote to Sir J.   1.10.1883, SMDC Patent Museum 6133 (copy).
    Donnelly

104 terse confidential report   SMDC. Science and Art 7205.n.d. (copy)

105 recommended himself   Stuart Wortley to Sir P. Owen (Cunliffe Owen)
                                 6.12.1883, SMDC, Science and Art, 7205 (copy).

106 the Treasury–Bramwell   Report, 27.7.1885.
    Committee

107 redeeming will   Agnes Bertha Woodcroft. 1903 (extract). SMDC, File 27,
                                 7157 AM.

146

14 The Library, origins to 1902

The Patent Law Amendment Act did not ordain a library for the new Office, but it implied one in the requirement to make patent records available for search. As already described, in the optimistic atmosphere of Woodcroft's audiences with the Prince Consort and the memorials from the mechanical engineers and others which followed, the library, like the Patent Museum became official policy. A key document was Woodcroft's letter to Colonel Grey[1], the Prince's secretary, after his first meeting:

> His Honour the Master of the Rolls Sir John Romilly on his return to town this day (15th of January, 1853) favoured me with an early interview during which I told him as directed by His Royal Highness all the conversation I had the honour to have with His Royal Highness on Wednesday last. His Honour entirely coincides in the views expressed by his Royal Highness as to the great practical advantage that would arise to the country from the formation of a library of the inventions of all nations with indices chronologically arranged of each class of invention and also from the establishment of an institution to contain machines and models. With a view to aid his Royal Highness in such important national works his Honour will give his most zealous efforts for their establishment.

Ironically in view of the later history of the Office funds, at this time Romilly believed[2] that a surplus "could not be more beneficially expended than in extending the knowledge of invention and thereby giving inventive talent a proper direction".

Evidently sensing a kindred spirit, Woodcroft continued with pardonable effusiveness for two and a half pages, enclosing a copy of *A Sketch of the Origin and Progress of Steam Navigation* and a specimen of his index. Romilly and Woodcroft had a later meeting with Prince Albert (Jan. 10, 1853) at which the library and Museum were discussed.

The day the Commissioners' servants (in Woodcroft's phrase) occupied the Masters' offices, he placed "a library of books and a large collection of mechanical models" there.[3] (It was also the day of Woodcroft's first Windsor audience, evidently a busy one.) Before the library opened, the

147

Office accounts for 1853 include "rent for two sets of rooms fitting for a library" in the main Office rent.

On March 9, 1855, *The Patent Journal* carried a notice that the Library (we can now give it a capital L) had opened the previous Monday, the 5th. It also reported the first donation, from Lady Bentham, widow of Sir Samuel Bentham (1757-1831), the naval architect, of several volumes of her husband's works. The Commissioners' report for 1854 (July 1855) noted, "the Commissioners have established a public library of research within the Patent Office in Southampton Buildings. Convenient rooms are provided for the purpose and the Library is open to the public from 10 to 4 every day". It was the nation's first free public science library and made a commensurate impression.

On the last day of March 1855 *The Mechanics' Magazine*[4] carried a short report, "Government Patent Office, Library and Reading room". At this early stage the Library's reading room stock was probably limited to its own publications, the indexes and *The Patent Journal* together with such published specifications as were available. The account added that "the Library likewise contains a number of volumes on general scientific subjects".

An early ground-plan of the offices published from a woodcut Woodcroft supplied to *The Engineer* in 1857 shows that the Library occupied the eastern half of the central vaulted corridor, the other half being a lobby, but also a larger rectangular chamber beyond, adjacent to Woodcroft's room. This was evidently the "room near Chancery Lane" of Dodd's report (Ch.6). The corridor, the notorious "drain pipe" was fitted with readers' tables between the cases of specifications. The remaining space was so narrow that a reader could only just squeeze between.

A visitor from *The Engineer,* complained:

> Where is it? Have any of our readers ever groped their way into this arcana of science? – this concentrated collection of all that is both new and old and curious in art – this store of new notions? Our duties have unfortunately compelled us to search for it, and by the exercise of those prominent virtues patience and perseverance we have been able after many turnings to reach its entrance and after many visits are beginning to know our way in…

Before reaching the door we have to pass through a lobby or antechamber specially intended as a resting place for umbrellas ... Upon the door of the Library being opened one is positively startled and seized with the same sort of feeling that is experienced when, in a dark room, one runs up against the edge of a door that was supposed to be shut. The effect of this is to involuntarily close the door again and wait for permission to enter: the impression being that the room is chock full and that you have arrived at a very inconvenient time ...

All this arises from the door as it opens, positively grazing the cases of specifications which you are thus compelled to rub against until fairly in. Now come both mental and bodily difficulties – to determine where the Library begins and where it ends – to determine where you are to stand, not to say sit – how you are to reach any case – how you can get even at the index which, lying on the table might be able to be easily accessible.

Other impressions (see Ch.6) of the "room near Chancery Lane" beyond the 7'6" wide "drain pipe" were more favourable.

The first relief was on April 23, 1857, when the former Chancery Sale Room on the first floor was opened as an addition to the Library. The accounts record[6], "Paid carpenter, joiner, painter and smith, for reconstructing and fitting up additions to the Library, £163 7s 10d".

In the Office annual staff returns, the Library is not treated separately until the 1870s; except for the Librarian, Atkinson, the staff are simply part of the specification staff. They all worked on the Office publications in addition to library duties. A window opens on the Library in early 1864, when Edmunds demanded a work-description[7] from all of them. They were four besides Atkinson: J.J.V. Elwin had started as an "extra clerk" in 1853 at £78 a year; he described "collating and arranging books, etc., and compiling manuscript indexes to same" as well as "assisting visitors to perfect their searches". (There were no published catalogues after Atkinson's of 1857-8, until the 1880s.) R.B. Prosser, already introduced, (Ch.7) included maintaining and progressing the periodicals and their catalogue and "assisting in the general business of the Library". H.J. Allison has been introduced (Ch.7), he was to be the second Librarian in the 1880s. Joseph Robert Morris, besides assisting

149

with the book catalogue, included "copying and transposing for alphabetical arrangement, the translated indexes of foreign periodicals". (Evidently the *Index to Foreign Scientific Periodicals* already described (Ch.6) was compiled for internal use before publication began in 1866.) The Messenger, "Padbury" also described his duties which included going out for refreshments. By 1878 the staff numbered seven, including two "attendants, 2nd class". Tolhausen the translator was included. Prosser had by then been moved to indexing and Elwin to specifications.

Only a few copies were printed of the first library catalogue[8] *of Books, Chiefly the Property of Mr Woodcroft*. It was stopped in order to include the Prosser books when eventually bought. The first truly published catalogue[9] appeared in two parts, in 1857 and 1858. It was compiled by Atkinson on the system of the Italian immigrant Andrea Crestadoro (1808-1879). He had studied in the British Museum Library and became Librarian of the Manchester City Library in 1862. His *The Art of Making Catalogues of Libraries* had been published in 1856; Atkinson's copy is still in the collections. The first volume of Atkinson's catalogue is a non-alphabetical numbered inventory, with some subject grouping; the second is an index to the first.

The larger part of the catalogue was taken up with the foundation collections of Woodcroft and the elder Prosser. The first intimation of the latter collection was when Woodcroft reported to Prince Albert[10] in January 1853 that it would be sent "immediately, on loan" until the Library could form its own.

Woodcroft's books, 388 titles, and Prosser's 707, both included likely items for a patent expert and a working engineer, such as manuals and reference books, but the considerable proportion of antiquarian titles in both made a strangely grand send-off for a Government library. Woodcroft's contained a modest thirteen titles pre-1800 and one or two of the 16th century, but Prosser's numbered 26 pre-1700, and no less than 173 published before 1800. Woodcroft's was strong in mathematics, shipbuilding and textile engineering. His long runs of *The Repertory of Art, The Mechanics' Magazine* and *Repertory of Patented Inventions* were of immediate value to the Library. Prosser's books, besides being more numerous and varied, were a bibliophile's dream, covering mathematics, millwork, geology, mining, railways, ordnance, pure science, agriculture, natural history and architecture. (It would be an interesting exercise to

150

work out how many are still in the British Library, after the Great Leap Forward and reorganisation of the science collections of the 1960s.)

Atkinson evidently cared about his catalogue, at least one biographical notice specially mentions it. Vol. l, the inventory volume, is a considerable achievement for a former lawyer and clerk; it has a fine rubricated title and painstaking transcriptions of long title pages, with translations from the Latin and Greek. The summaries of contents of multi-volume works such as John Bowring's first collected edition of Jeremy Bentham (1838-42) take up at least half a page per volume. Eyre and Spottiswoode also used a variety of type, to aid presentation. However, it would be interesting to know what the average Patent Office reader (if there is such) would have made of many of the texts.

The making-over of these two collections was a generous gesture in keeping with the idealistic origins of the Library and Museum. There was some tension between the cataloguer and his superior. Woodcroft requested a footnote on the first page stating that his collection "led to the institution of the Free Public Library". Atkinson pencilled underneath in the Library copy, "the copy for this note was supplied by Mr Woodcroft and its insertion insisted upon, notwithstanding the protest of the Librarian. The statement is not true".

Was it the proportion of pre-1800 works that led William Spence, a patent agent, to write to *Aris's Birmingham Gazette* in 1857, "there is an important practical difference between a mere antiquarian collection, containing curious, perhaps often absurd inventions, and one dealing with sound and valuable inventions". W.C. Aitken replied, pointing out that Woodcroft could be relied on to know what was appropriate, and that discouraging potential donors at this early stage might impoverish the Library. With an uncertain budget the Library was undoubtedly weak in new books in the early years. In 1864 the consulting engineer E.A. Cowper told the Library and Museum enquiry[11], "the modern books are not all there; for instance the first and second volumes of some books are there, but not the third and fourth. You go for... any books published last year and there is not a chance of getting it. I have a list of fifty first-rate scientific books that you cannot get there".

This was a period when the progress of the "free library" was watched by a wide range of daily and specialist press. In June 1855, *The Builder*

151

stressed[12] the value of specifications to the architect; the principal advantage of the new publishing regime was in having the nucleus of a library, and attributed the improved arrangements to Woodcroft.

In May 1855 *The Morning Advertiser*[13] reported that "presentations from various quarters have already reached the hand of the librarian", and *The Law Times*[14] hoped that liberal donations would follow. In Atkinson's catalogue, nos 1094-1827 are donations, led by the United States official patent publications. Among the more than a score of donors were the Italian Patent Office, the Franklin Institute, the University of New York, the governments of Prussia, Austria, Bavaria and Brazil; of UK official bodies, the Record Commissioners, Admiralty, the India and War Offices and the Registrar General. The private donors, as noted, included Lady Bentham. The Cambridge University Press gave a number of theological works, which like a large donation from the East India Company, were disposed of later. There is no published record between 1857 and 1883, but Woodcroft told the 1864 Library and Museum enquiry[15] that the Library then held some 30,000 volumes.

Before the Edmunds affair became public, in 1863, press complaints at the state of the Library almost certainly inspired by leaks from the Office, blamed Edmunds for the lack of funding. In a Parliamentary return requested by the vigilant Mr Dillwyn and largely concerned with compensation being paid to redundant legal staff, the information required included the duties and days of attendance of the Clerk of the Commissioners. In a heavily ironic description of Edmunds' various sources of income, *The Colliery Guardian*[16] commented:

> Content with his own small salary, as we believe he is, and fully conscious of the excess of the salaries of the superintendent of specifications and chief clerk respectively, considering their subordinate duties and responsibilities he wished in some way to reduce the current expenses of the Office and therefore curtailed the supply of books and periodicals...

This period, with the library stock growing and before the relief of the 1866/7 rebuilding, conditions were at their worst. After alluding to the achievements of the "earnest and judicious officer, Bennet Woodcroft", *The Mechanics' Magazine* continued[17]:

the delay in obtaining a suitable building for the library is bringing disgrace upon the whole system. The present apartment is about three or four yards square. It would be considered by most persons too small to put half-a-dozen clerks in and yet it is deemed proper to continue to use it as a public library and that too of the most important character; for there is not a class library in England of so much importance or which should be of so much importance as the library for inventors. The room does not contain a tithe of the volumes which the Commissioners already have, although the walls are covered with books, the tables heaped with indexes and the floor paved with specifications. Persons (some of whom are ladies) come to the place, often from afar, open the door, look in with bewilderment upon a little crowd of individuals elbowing each other's sides, closing each other's books, sweeping away each other's papers and apologising all round and they turn away disappointed and annoyed.

As a partial response to the recommendations of the 1864 Commons report, in 1865 the Chancellor, Lord Chelmsford, suggested[18] that Pennethorne be asked to estimate the cost of adding a new library to the existing Masters' offices on the upper floor at roof level.(The remaining Chancery staff were to move to the new Strand Law Courts.) In July that year he was authorised to proceed[19] with designing a library with a fireproof floor intended to cost £8,800. In December 1866 he recommended adding five more rooms, but these had to wait until the 1880s.

Pennethorne's biographer[20] has written:

> The new library was planned like a basilica, with an arched nave of four bays containing the readers' desks, flanked by 'aisles' containing the bookcases. There were offices at either end of the room. There was no embellishment outside....The semicircular-arched roof rested on 'piers' articulated by Corinthian 'columns' with windows in the roof space over the frieze. Here however the material was wrought iron.... Iron had already been used in a number of the great libraries of the 19th century, notably Labrouste's Bibliothèque Ste Geneviève in Paris and Sydney Smirke's British Museum Reading Room. While lacking the grandeur and excitement of these much larger buildings Pennethorne's library at the Patent Office was a

153

characteristically competent building at low cost. There was a certain amount of colour and ornament.... It cost some £15,000.

This first purpose-built space for the Office opened on April 16, 1867[21]. Architectural description can be compared with visitor's impressions The period's love of colour is evident from the unfairly tetchy account in *The Engineer*[22], after a preview:

Yesterday we made an inspection of the place after the fearful task of ascending fifty two stone steps. In the long ascent the aid of the hand-rail was required. A worse specimen of handrails in general we never met with in a public building. It is of mahogany, 2.5 in. square very plainly moulded set on square iron balustrades such as are generally used in prison... We beheld the vestibule, 21 ft by 14 ft 3 in. leading to another vestibule. In this our eyes first encountered the tiled floor composed of inferior quarries, red and buff. We then entered the library before us, but instead of a chaste and beautiful room we found ourselves within a building having all the appearances of a country music hall designed by an amateur, after the bricklayer's order of architecture.

After describing unfavourably the iron-columned *salon* he continues with the decoration:

The whole of the upper part of the walls and inside of the roofing are covered with a barbarous imitation of fresco painting. This part of the decoration was evidently done with stencils and, like the well known 'willow pattern plate', all the patterns match... Around the walls under the upper windows are a number of rectangular panels surrounded by 'rope borders. These are evidently intended for the names of eminent persons... The door at the extreme end leads to the room set apart for *The Times* and another room for books. The floors to which we have already referred ought at least to have been of Minton's encaustic tiles of elegant design... The columns are painted, base black, surbase maroon or chocolate; the stem white and capitals white relieved with red. The base and surbase of the walls are similarly painted and if they are permitted to remain of this colour will have a good effect. The arches are bedecked with gold and colours of many hues, the ground being white. We must add that the carpentry is excellent

The report concluded that while greatly superior to the ground-floor accommodation "the whole affair is insignificant, paltry and unsuitable to the purpose intended, and unworthy of the great resources of the Patent Office". At least it threw light on the period's expectations as to public buildings.

This was to be the Library's home for more than thirty years.

Despite the wretched conditions of the first library, reader numbers grew steadily from a modest 2,500 for the nine months of 1855, by some 1,500 a year up to 13,000 in 1866 before the new reading room opened. In 1867-8 there was a surge to 17,500. The Commissioners Report for 1870 stated, "The Library has greatly increased and continues to increase, partly by purchase but in a great measure by gifts and loans of valuable and useful books...it has become a collection of great interest and importance". From its beginning the Library was very conscious of reader numbers[23], keeping a meticulous record and publishing occasional tables of figures in *The Patent Journal*. It also kept grand totals; by the end of the century more than two million had crossed its threshold, and figures were maintained into the 1930s.

The internationalist ideals of the Exhibition period certainly influenced acquisitions policy until the pressure to specialisation in science and technology in the 20th century. Donations certainly contributed to the liberal character of the collection but so did acquisition. (In the 1860s there was an unsuccessful attempt to buy a copy of Audubon's *Birds of America*.) Many minor donations were made by the patent community of readers, lawyers and agents and were recorded periodically in the *Journal*. Unfortunately expenditure was hidden in the stationery account; in 1871 the Office spent £1,737 (equivalent £86,000) on stationery including binding.

In the absence of systematic library reports under the Commissioners, Library history is inevitably a matter of intermittent glimpses. The first published catalogue to follow Atkinson's after an interval of more than twenty years, the 1881-3 volumes[24] were published without prefatory matter. It lists some 14,000 titles.

In 1897 E.W. Hulme who had joined in 1881, like Housman, as a Higher Division clerk and succeeded Allison as Librarian in 1894, described the

Library in the 19th century in an address to the Library Association[25]. It was, he said, perhaps better appreciated abroad than in the UK. At the time he spoke the Library was just introducing his own "minute system of classification which to some extent renders the student independent of catalogues and staff" and was particularly designed for the scientific researcher – it is of course still in use in modified form. He said that the 1883 stock had doubled by the end of the century. He singled out certain 19th century acquisitions such as the Norman Collection of aeronautical prints and the Koning Collection on printing history – and printing mythology.

In his guide *London Past and Present* (1891) R.B. Wheatley described the Library as "the only really free library in London". Free it was, but lack of space and consequently of facilities caused dissatisfaction among professional users. In two addresses to the Institute of Patent Agents[26] in 1884 and 1891, P. Jensen complained of the inadequate indexes and abridgments (the new technical staff had not yet made up the arrears), the late arrival of foreign patent data and the lack of up to date textbooks. He pointed out that Britain made lavish, prompt donations to foreign institutions compared with their niggardly response. At the end of the century a correspondent to *The Engineer*[27] criticised the general quality of the stock, making unfavourable comparisons with a copyright library such as the British Museum, to which R.B. Prosser replying in retirement pointed out its strengths in foreign literature.

Pennethorne's upstairs library with some additional rooms had to serve until the 1890s, when at last the government took steps to provide a great manufacturing nation with the Patent Office and Library it deserved. The decision to develop on the same general location was in keeping with the choice of the 1864 committee and the United Inventors Association. The Office was rebuilt[28] in stages between 1893 and 1912, encroaching on the properties – some of them slummy – to the south (Tooks Court) and east of the old Masters' offices, occupying the sites of 27 and 28 Southampton Buildings and others of Staple Inn. The Library block and existing (1998) frontage on Southampton Buildings were built between 1898 and 1902; by the end of 1900 the Library lacked only its steel and glass roof. Early briefing for the architect, Sir John Taylor (1833-1912), an assistant once of Pennethorne, whose influence is apparent, was provided by H.J. Allison the Librarian (d. 1894) and then by E.W. Hulme. Library service continued during this

156

difficult time from Bishop's Court on the west side of Chancery Lane. Hulme's surviving file[29] reveals his detailed overseeing of the fitting out of the new library. It opened in January 1902.

A large increase in examining staff on the introduction of the search for novelty in 1904 required more expansion: in 1903 finance was granted under statute (3 Edw.VII c.41) for an easterly extension with a new Furnival St entrance, opened in 1907. Stylistically, historicism prevailed for the new Office; the formal frontages of the new buildings all followed the fluted-pilasters, mullioned Tudor style of the Chancery Taxing Masters' building of 1843 facing Staple Inn garden which was destroyed in the Second World War.

At the end of the century the Library had a staff of 11. The middle of rebuilding was not a good time for a new publishing venture but it proved its vitality by one of its most successful. The Comptroller's Report for 1900 announced that "a series of small handbooks designed to serve as guides to the content of the Library are now in course of preparation". No 1 was a *Key to Classification of French Patent Specifications* and No 2 was a popular subject list covering photography. This Patent Office Library Series of duodecimo (pocketbook) paperback guides had a wider and more favourable reception even than the Office's earliest publications. A classified library was still a novelty, and specialist journals of all kinds[30] hailed this new facility for the searcher with limited time and subject field. The wheel had come full circle from Woodcroft's enthusiastic advocacy of classification in his meetings with Prince Albert.

The late 19th century and years before the Great War saw the first recognition of the scientific information explosion. (The Royal Society's *Catalogue of Scientific Papers* was partly compiled in the Patent Office Library). In its new building it was able to make up for the earlier lean years. In a statement to the Swan Committee[31] in 1944 the Librarian, F.W. Gravell, reported that holdings had virtually doubled between 1901 and 1920. The Library had a cherished place as a national institution and an international reputation. To choose one among several notices in French and German, *La Revue Technique*[32] in 1904 reviewed the Library Series No 14, *Electricity, Magnetism and Electrotechnics*:

La Bibliothèque de l'Office des Brevets anglais possedait la plupart des ouvrages scientifiques qui se publient, la consultation de ce catalogue rendra des services non seulement à tous ceux qui frequentent cette bibliothèque, mais encore à tous ceux qui desirent se renseigner rapidement sur l'existence d'ouvrages traitant une question speciale. Aussi est-il à souhaiter que la publication de catalogues de ce genre se généralise, et q'en particulier les conservateurs de nos grandes bibliothèques françaises parviennent à en livrer à un prix aussi modique.

The Library of the Office of English Patents holds most published scientific works. Consulting this catalogue will help not only those who use this library, but also those who want to be able to learn quickly about the existence of works treating specialist subjects. Moreover we hope that the publication of catalogues of this type will become more widespread, and in particular the curators of our great French libraries will manage to produce such catalogues at a reasonable price.

Notes to Chapter 14

1 Woodcroft's letter to Col. Grey — Royal Archives, 5.1.1853.

2 Romilly believed — Ibid.

3 he placed "a library of books and a large collection of mechanical models" — Woodcroft, *Minute Brook.* Transcript, BLRIS SC.

4 *The Mechanics' Magazine* — **62**, 31.3.1855, p.297.

5 a visitor from *The Engineer* — 14.11.1856, p.626.

6 The accounts record — Commissioners' Report, 1857.

7 a work-description — BLSRIS SC Woodcroft Coll., MS 22.1.1864.

8 first Library catalogue — 1856. BLSRIS SC.

9 The first published catalogue — *Catalogue of the Library of the Great Seal Patent Office*, 2pt London, Queen's Printers, 1857, 1858.

10 reported to Prince Albert — 21.1.1853, Royal Archives. F.25.

11 Cowper told the Library & Museum enquiry — Minutes, 14.6.1864. Q. 719.

12 *The Builder* stressed — 23.6.1855, 289-90.

13 *The Morning Advertiser* — 9.8.1855.

14 *The Law Times* 5.5.1855.

15 Woodcroft told the 1864 Minutes. 7.6.1864, Q.252.
Library and Museum
enquiry

16 *The Colliery Guardian* 12.4.1863.

17 *The Mechanics' Magazine* ?.11.1856 (reprinted).

18 Lord Chelmsford, Tyack, G. *Sir James Pennethorne* as cited (see Ch.4), p.275.
suggested

19 was authorised to proceed Ibid.

20 Pennethorne's biographer Ibid.

21 opened on April 16, 1867 Commissioners' Report, 1867, p.9.

22 tetchy account in *The* **22**, 5.10.1866, p.267.
Engineer

23 reader numbers File, BLSRIS SC.

24 1881–1883 Catalogue *Catalogue of the Library of the Patent Office. Arranged alphabetically and by Subject.* 2 vol. London, 1881,1883.

25 an address to the Library *English Patent Law, its History Literature and Library. Read*
Association *at the 20th Annual Meeting of the Library Association.* London 1898.

26 two addresses to the *The Patent Office Library; a Few Notes on the Patent Office*
Institute of Patent Agents *Library,* London, Spottiswoode, 1884. 1891.

27 a correspondent to *The* 9.12.1898.
Engineer

28 The Office was rebuilt Harding, pp.33–36. Comptroller's Reports, 1898–1912. *The Builder,* 18.1.1902; Caswell, Brian', POESM 183, 11.1975.

29 Hulme's surviving file BLSRIS SC.

30 specialist journals of all *Patent Office Library Series. Reviews and other Notices.*
kinds BLSRIS SC (scrapbook).

31 a statement to the Typescript. BLSRIS SC.
Swan Committee

32 *La Revue Technique* **19**, 15.10.1904.

Appendix I: Patent office staff

ADMINISTRATION AND STAFF, APRIL 1880

GREAT SEAL PATENT OFFICE, OFFICE OF THE
COMMISSIONERS OF PATENTS FOR INVENTIONS,
DESIGNS REGISTRY, AND TRADE MARKS REGISTRY.

25, SOUTHAMPTON BUILDINGS, CHANCERY LANE, W.C.

COMMISSIONERS OF PATENTS FOR INVENTIONS.

The Right Honourable The Lord High Chancellor.
The Right Honourable The Master of the Rolls.
The Attorney-General, M.P., Q.C.
The Solicitor-General, M.P., Q.C.

Clerk of the Commissioners – – –   H. Reader Lack.
Private Secretary to Clerk of Commissioners   W. M. Michell.

PATENT OFFICE

PATENT BRANCH.

Principal –   –   –   –   –   R. Lucas.
First Class Clerk   –   –   –   A. C. Forrester.
Second Class Clerks –   –   –   S. S. Tripp, A. J. White, E. Towers.
Third Class Clerk   –   –   –   G. Spencer.
Higher Division Clerk   –   –   Vacant.
Extra Clerks –   –   –   –   G. Stanford, C. Lever, A. Towers.
Lower Division Clerks   –   –   W. H. Cheffins, J. G. Walker, jun,
                                     F. Sawyer, J. R. Sturt, jun,
                                     W. H. Crossley.

3 Copyists.

PRINTING AND DRAWINGS BRANCH.

Principal - - - - -	J. J. V. Elwin.
Second Class Clerk - - -	H. S. H. Pegler.
Extra Clerk - - - -	S. Casserley.
Lower Division Clerks - -	V. I. Feeney, J. H. H. Peake, T. F. Ordish.

2 Copyists.

INDEXING BRANCH.

Principal - - - - -	J. F. Flack.
Second Class Clerk - - -	J. S. S. Escott, B. A.
Lower Division Clerks - -	H. E. D. Jones, T. Press.

1 Copyist.
1 Boy Copyist.

SPECIAL INDEXING BRANCH.

First Class Clerk - - -	R. B. Prosser.
Second Class Clerk - - -	F. W. Tabrum.
Indexing Clerks - - - -	J. M. H. Munro, D.Sc., J. Gray, B Sc., H. Hatfield, A. Cliff, A. J. Walke, W. Martin.

ABRIDGMENTS BRANCH.

Principal - - - - -	W. M. Michell.
Second Class Clerk - - -	G. H. Hardy.
Third Class Clerk - - -	J. Maycock.
Lower Division Clerks - -	T. Ridge, F. W. Neale.

FREE LIBRARY.

Librarian - - - - -	W. G. Atkinson.
Translator - - - - -	A. Tolhausen.
Second Class Clerk - - -	H. J. Allison, M. Collinson.
Lower Division Clerk - -	H. Lennane.
Attendants, Second Class - -	E. Collins, A. Thomas

SALE AND STORE BRANCH.

Superintendent - - - - J. R. Morris.
Cash Clerk - - - - J. R. Sturt, sen.
Extra Clerk - - - - J. E. Doewra.
2 Copyists.
Warehousekeeper - - - E. Harris.
Warehousemen - - - - W. J. Philips, F. Falkner,
A. Mount, W. Carpenter,
G. Taylor.

COPYING BRANCH.

6 Copyists.

PATENT MUSEUM.
(South Kensington.)

Superindent - - - - H. Reader Lack.
Curator - - - - - Lt.-Col. A. H. P. Stuart-Wortley.
Assistant to Curator - - - J. T. Scott.
Lower Division Clerk- - - W. R. Swain.
Machinist - - - - - S. Ford.
Pattern Maker and Joiner - - G. Moore.
Assistant Machinist - - - J. Hill.
Attendent, First Class - - - H. Phelps.
Attendents, Second Class - - E. Vowles, A. Fairbrass,
H. S. Hunt.

1 Boy Messenger

DESIGNS REGISTRY.

Registrar - - - - - H. Reader Lack.
Assistant Registrar - - - J. L. Whittle, M. A.
Second Class Clerk - - - R. D. Spinks.
Third Class Clerks - - - B. Tall, S. H. C. Kingsford.
1 Copyist.
Printer and Messenger - - R. Radwell.

162

TRADE MARKS REGISTRY

Registrar - - - - -	H. Reader Lack.
Assistant Registrar - - -	J. L. Whittle, M. A.
Second Class Clerk - - -	W. J. F. Tomlinson.
Third Class Clerks - - -	T. W. H. Davies, E. T. Kingsford (temporarily).
Higher Division Clerk - -	F. W. Hodges.
Compositor of Trade - - - Marks Journal, &c.	C. Thomas.
Lower Division Clerks - -	E. Sawyer, W. E. Milliken, H. Millyard, J. Stringer, E. H. Knights.

8 Copyists.

TRADE MARKS REGISTRY, BRANCH OFFICE.

(18 Royal Exchange, Manchester.)

Keeper - - - - -	J. Fry.
Assistant - - - - -	J. W. Madders.

4 Sorters.
1 Messenger.

FINANCE

Financial Clerk - - - -	A. J. Rhodes.
Lower Division Clerk- - -	A. H. Lobban.

Office Keeper.

Messengers, First Class - -	J. W. Padbury, J. H. Foster, G. Jenkins, A. W. Elsmore.
Messengers, Second Class - -	C. Hayes, J. Hayes.
Fireman - - - - -	G. I. Turner.

1 Boy Messenger.

April, 1880.

Index

HOW TO FIND INFORMATION:
PATENTS ON THE INTERNET
by David Newton

A wealth of information about patents has recently been made available on the Internet as patent offices and other organisations have launched new services. Whether you are a newcomer to searching patents or an old hand, this short guide gives you details of many important Internet sources. One section describes the key free databases and compares them with added value resources. Increasingly, helpful tools, such as patent classification schemes and tutorials, are being put on the Internet and, where useful, these are referenced. As with the rest of the Internet, the patent sites are constantly changing but users of the book will have the option of updating references through the British Library's own patent pages. Dr Newton is Head of the British Library Patent Information service.

Forthcoming 2000, Price £9.95 (overseas postage extra)
Paperback, approx 40 pages, 210x146mm, ISBN 0-7123-0864-4

To order: please see overleaf.

INTRODUCTION TO PATENTS INFORMATION
3^(RD) edition
edited by Stephen van Dulken

This guide is a practical step-by-step introduction to searching for UK and overseas patent information. Topics covered include: official printed data sources, online and CD-ROM databases, patent classification and legislation. The guide covers patent searching worldwide but with particular emphasis on the UK and the rest of Europe, Japan and the USA. Beginners will find that it gives them a complete introduction to patent searching, while more experienced searchers will find the text a useful refresher. The author works in the British Library Patent Information Service.

'It is a valuable reference source for anyone who needs to search for patents on technology.'
New Scientist, about the 2^(ND) edition

Publication 1998, Price £32.00 (overseas postage extra)
Paperback, 121 pages, 297x210mm, ISBN 0-7123-0838-5

To order: please see overleaf.

BRITISH PATENTS OF INVENTION, 1617-1977: A GUIDE FOR RESEARCHERS
by Stephen van Dulken

This unique guide explains how researchers can use patents as a source of historical information. Covering the British patents system from 1617 until the 1977 Patents Act, the guide is an invaluable resource for anyone researching the history of science and technology or looking for information on the people behind the inventions. Sections include: the historical background of the patent system, patenting procedure, people in the patent system, the patent specifications, and searching for patents information.

'It should be in every public and private patent and historical library resource.'
World Patent Information

Published 1999. Price £39.00 (overseas postage extra)
Paperback, 211 pages, 297x210mm, ISBN 0-7123-0817-2

Orders to: Turpin Distribution Services Ltd, Blackhorse Road, Letchworth, Herts SG6 1HN, UK. Tel +44(0)1462 672555, Fax +44(0)1462 480947, Email turpin@rsc.org
USA and Canada: University of Toronto Press, 5201 Dufferin Street, Downsview, Ontario, M3H 5T8 Canada. Tel 416 667 7791, Fax 416 667 7832, Email utpbooks@utpress.utoronto.ca